HEART MANAGEMENT

Declutter Your Heart, Declutter Your Life

ANGELA CARWHEEL, MACE, MTS

Praise for Heart Management

"***Heart Management*** is a breath of fresh air for anyone longing to find clarity, courage, and spiritual renewal in the everyday grind of life. Angela's warmth and authenticity seeps through as she combines biblical insight with practical steps for emotional and spiritual health. This is truly a book that can help the reader make a positive and lasting impact on their family and community."

—J.W. Mackey, author of *Weary Wanderers*

"With gentle honesty and practical wisdom, Angela Carwheel gathers the scattered pieces of everyday faith and lays them before the reader, inviting us to pause and reflect on the shape of our hearts. This book is a quiet companion…honest, warm, and rooted in grace…guiding each of us toward hope and wholeness, one tender step at a time."

—Zach Anderson, author and missionary

"Angela is a consummate professional. Her work is impressive. Even though her expertise is primarily in encouraging women, the principles she develops will work for everyone who needs a "nudge" in the right direction."

—Greg Zhelezny, author of *Parables of Christ*

"Angela Carwheel's ***Heart Management*** encourages readers to pause, reflect, and realign emotionally and spiritually. This book offers the reader hope and direction for the journey ahead."

— Nadine Joubert-Robinson
Founder and Director TRANSFORM Consultancy

Heart Management / Angela Carwheel,
Excel Life Coaching for Women, LLC

ISBN Hardback: 979-8-9993983-0-7
ISBN Paperback: 979-8-9993983-1-4

Library of Congress Control Number:
2025921141

DISCLAIMER
This book shares life coaching insights and biblical counseling tips meant to encourage and inspire. It is not professional counseling, therapy, or medical advice. For personal challenges, please seek guidance from a licensed professional or trusted spiritual leader.

Printed in the United States of America

www.excellifecoachingforwomen.com

In memory of Tee~
We laughed. We cried. We stumbled. We shared. We were authentic. Although *Heart Management* is not about you, you sought to deal with the intricate parts of your heart realizing that nothing is hidden from the Lord. You desired a life that would be pleasing to Him. I will forever miss you, my dearest youngest sister, but I look forward to the day when our Lord will appear, and we will meet each other in the air, and thus we will always be together with the Lord (2 Thess. 4:16-17). Your memory will never depart from my heart.

Heart Management is dedicated to my deceased God-fearing parents, Archie and Ruth Washington. Although home with Jesus, I am continually reminded of your dedication and fervent spirit of compassion, love, grace, and faith to everyone you encountered. I long to see you once again!

Additionally, Dorothy Mae Ballard, my dearest godmother, I will always cherish your memory. The last section in *Heart Management* comprises the acronym, "F-R-E-E-D-OM." You exhibited this word profoundly! The D stands for Dignity. I dedicate this section to you. Your smile stands still within my heart.

I give honor
to my Lord
and Savior
Jesus Christ.
You have made everything possible
in my life. Thank you for the journey
that You have allowed me to travel.
My heart says, please the Lord,
and I desire
to do just that.
Without You,
I am nothing!

Greg, Genesis, and Alexander:
Your love for Jesus, prayer, support, patience, and encouragement have made what seemed impossible, possible! I value your various perspectives, temperaments, and gifts. You all are my inspiration. Greg, listed in the last section of *Heart Management* are tips stated through the acronym: F-R-E-E-D-O-M. The section on "Manage Your Time" is dedicated to you. You have learned to weigh your moments and maximize your time to impact others' lives. I praise my God, daily, for your leadership in our family.

~I love you dearly and forever!

To my wonderful father-in-law and mother-in-law, Ed and Ellen Carwheel. You have consistently demonstrated a strong dependence on the Lord. Your exemplary example of Christ's love through prayer, support, and perseverance has blessed His people.

~I praise my God every time I think about you!

Pastor Hal Hopkins, I appreciate the support you have provided me throughout the many years I have known you. "Impact" and rising above natural thinking patterns have challenged me to move fearlessly and trust God in the process of life. I am always reminded in my relationship with the Lord that everything in life begins with the heart.

~Thank you!

CONTENTS

"Life is about accepting the challenges along the way, choosing to keep moving forward, and savoring the journey."

In May 2025, while in a self-publishing class for ministry, my peers and I had to compile documents from our personal files that we had previously written. This compilation of at least seventy-five pages would ultimately become a non-fiction manuscript for publishing. I thought, "I have that!" However, I had not organized these files for manuscript perfection and publication, but I took on the task. It was not until well into the project that I realized this was the beginning of a challenging feat. I pulled together blogs and devotionals I had written years ago. Still, I prayed and continued the process. At this point, there was no turning back. With each deadline met and the idea of republishing after the class has ended, I became settled in heart, and this is how *Heart Management* was born.

I am thankful to Dr. Glann for teaching Self-Publishing for Ministry. Your insights, experience, and expertise have challenged my perspective on producing a worthwhile product to the glory of our Lord. It is the beginning of new ventures in my life.

INTRODUCTION

Has it been difficult to manage and maintain a heart centered on God? Do you ever take the time to assess your heart? No, there is not a form to complete, or a session needed for documentation, but think about the time it takes before you recognize that a heart change is needed?

Are you frustrated about a situation that you have yet to confront? Are you stressed about unresolved issues at work? Has someone else been given the job that you thought you deserved to get? Has someone taken advantage of your kindness at church? Has someone insulted your intelligence in school? Are you dealing with a physical ailment that is taking a toll on your life? Have you grieved a close family member or a dear friend, yet still have unresolved issues in your heart? Have you been tested to the core in your home? Or by friends? Family? How about enemies?

Yes, you have Jesus, but considering all the tests you have been through, has it made you bitter or disheartened? How about apathetic? Is your heart divided, torn between God and people? Or, are you experiencing God's peace and the security of knowing Him? Are you laying down your will and weights to accomplish His will? Is it time to stop and check your emotional heart for management of soul and spirit?

Have you asked the Lord to search your heart to ensure spiritual well-being? He is speaking to my heart even now! Yes, as I continue to utter words on paper from my heart, to your heart. We are on a journey, passing through this dear life that God has permitted. Our broken hearts, shaped by adversity, are in conflict between soul and spirit, but we must take the time to hear from the Lord to experience the life He came to bring.

Yes, we talk to Him, sharing our concerns, but waiting and listening to His voice in all matters of life is most difficult. When life stretches us through trials, disappointments, grief, anxiety, depression, brokenness, worry, illness, and just the pressure it brings, we must remember that we are not alone. God is present.

Proverbs 4:23 says, "Keep your heart with all diligence, for out of it *spring* the issues of life." "…The heart is the depository of all wisdom, and the source of whatever affects life and character" (Mt 12:35; 15:19). From the heart flows pride, frustration, resentment, jealousy, anger, fear, selfishness, deceit, greed, envy, unforgiveness, apathy, restlessness, and much more. Scripture warns us to confront these heartfelt deceptive traits, so that our lives will be changed and formed by Jesus' life.

God will reveal the mechanics and help you to assess your present state, gaps, needs, and next steps.

Would you rather experience God's love, joy, peace, and further faith in the difficulty, knowing that He can be trusted to work it out? We cling to God's heart because He is reliable, irreplaceable, and irresistible. He allows our depravity to reveal our inconsistencies, deficiencies, and irresponsibility. As David cried out to the Lord to search his heart for an in-depth assessment, we too must ask the Lord to reveal what is in our hearts, ensuring the right attitude, intentions, thoughts, and behavior. Managing one's heart, God's way, requires the

Holy Spirit's prompting and a rendering to His will. Jesus states, "Apart from Me, you can do nothing!"

Heart Management seeks to help individuals become aware of their whole-hearted need for total dependence on God. No matter what twists and turns we face in life, and no matter what we feel, Scripture teaches us that God is dependable, and His promises are true.

Heart Management encourages Christ-centered living as one takes steps to declutter his or her heart and pursue a purpose-filled life. It includes questions to consider and journaling to write down your thoughts as you ponder how the Lord is speaking to your heart. Throughout the pages of this book, ask yourself the question, Is my heart aligned with God's will? If your heart is aligned with God's will, stay there. Continue your journey, but always leave enough room for a heart evaluation. God will reveal the mechanics and help you to assess your present state, gaps, needs, and next steps. He makes known the paths of life, as His joy remains in our hearts. "You will show me the path of life; in Your presence is fullness of joy; at Your right hand are pleasures forevermore" (Ps. 16:11).

Before you move any further, ask the Lord to help rid yourself of all other voices or noise, including the person closest to you. Give the bare minimum, if needed. Confusion arises when we try to hear from God but keep allowing other voices to distort His leading in our lives. Next, ask the Lord to speak to your heart, by His Spirit, so that you will perceive exactly what He is saying. He may speak through a Scripture read, a message, a circumstance, or through people. As He reveals what's in your heart, confess and confront what He brings to your attention, and walk cautiously. Paul says, "walk circumspectly" (Eph. 5:15). Whatever He says to declutter, do it. Never wait until you are ready, because you can face a pile-up or an ambush of issues in your heart. Then you will be in danger of losing who you are, in soul and in spirit. You can harm your entire body if you deprive yourself of managing your heart.

We should never forget, "Clutter is not just the stuff on your floor; it's anything that stands between you and the life you want to be living." If you declutter your heart, you will also declutter your life.

Heart Management draws on specific aspects of my personal life story and on other stories that reflect God's goodness, grace, promises, and unmatched love. I give you a common place to begin where you can reflect, consider, and journal what is necessary to inspire righteous living.

Heart Management is expressed in four parts.

Part I, "Life Redirection," conveys the emotional heart that can become cluttered through life's unresolved and traumatic experiences. However, through reflection and renewed purpose, God gives wisdom, security, peace, and deepens our faith. Included are life tips, stories, and biblical inspiration for spiritual renewal and encouragement.

Part II, "Life Rip Currents," symbolizes the ups and downs we go through in life, and the questions we ask the Lord in need of understanding, fulfillment, and peace. Even though life can be complex, God provides insight and wisdom as we face dissatisfying circumstances. These events reinforce God's love through spiritual development and wholeness. In this section, you will find questions to consider, and for journal writing.

Part III covers "Life Reassuring Anchors," which are tidbits from God's Word that speak of God as our living Anchor who holds our future. In Him we live, move, and breathe. Questions to consider and for journaling have also been added to this section. So, continue to be thoughtful. Be inspired. Be challenged. Be exceptional. Be courageous. Be wise. Be motivated. Be encouraged. Be filled with the Spirit. Be spent (2 Cor. 12:15).

Part IV, "Life Refreshment," is broken down into an acronym, F-R-E-E-D-O-M. The word "freedom" is a goal most human beings desire. Freedom in Christ allows one to repurpose his or her life and experience God's compassion and spiritual blessings. The F is for Faith, R is for Recognize, E is for Engagement, the second E is for Endurance, D is for Dignity, O is for Opportunity, and M is for Management of Time. By God's Spirit, we experience the freedom to live in wisdom, acceptance, and confidence, knowing that it is God who has called us, and not we ourselves. As our hearts are being changed, others will be motivated toward change.

My prayer for you is twofold:
1. That you will take responsibility for your heart and allow God to fill you with His good pleasures
2. That you will join into a supportive community of godly people for accountability and further perspective in heart and mind

May you be filled with the love and warmth of God's Spirit and the peace, hope and joy of His forever presence.

Keep in mind:
"A heart aligned with God
is a life aligned with purpose."
~Unknown

Take heart and be encouraged,
~Angela

HEART MANAGEMENT

Declutter Your Heart, Declutter Your Life

Angela Carwheel MACE, MTS

PART I
LIFE REDIRECTION

"Create in me a clean heart, O God, and renew a steadfast spirit within me" (Ps. 51:10).

Chapter 1

THE HEART

My heart sank when our father went home to be with the Lord in January 1980. It shook our home and rocked our world. He loved God, family, church, and ministering to this broken world. He was a very busy man but maximized his time on purpose. He was a leading local and radio pastor, and a biblical counselor through the radio waves within the Pennsylvania tri-state area. Thirty-eight years old, working on a master's degree and thriving in life, but God sent a rip current into the lives of many people who loved and respected him.

A month and a half earlier, he had taken my eldest sister and I out shopping in downtown Philadelphia. It was a Saturday morning, in December 1979. When we left the house with Dad, he securely held our hands as we walked down Seymour Street in Germantown, PA. We were walking toward the trolley stop on Germantown Avenue. The excitement was surreal, and we were at peace, because our dad was with us. Not a worry or concern, as his heavenly father loved and protected him, my sister and I felt

Not a worry or concern, as his heavenly father loved and protected him, we felt his love and protection.

his love and protection. Prior to this extraordinary day, Dad had prepared all six of his children for an outing of two with him. So, the excitement increased when the first two of us left our home. As early as I could remember, his face had shone the inner joy expressed from his heart. It was the joy of the Lord. Even when he was not smiling, he was thoughtful.

We had gone to the Big Man's Store. Yes, he was a big guy and wore it well! The awareness he exuded of God was magnetic. As he led, we followed. He was trustworthy because He trusted in the One who gave him life. When we entered the Big Man's Store, they immediately addressed his needs as if this was not the first time they had met him. They apparently had known him from previous visits because they greeted him with respect and gratitude to see him again.

The awareness he exuded of God was magnetic, so as he led, we followed.

We smiled as he introduced us to every familiar face. It was beyond our scope as they measured him for a new suit. It was not just any kind of suit. It was an indigo jean suit. This was unusual because we had never seen our dad in an indigo jean suit. Every suit he had worn up until this point was the typical conservative black, navy, or gray. He was a man of class, and integrity. I must say, the jean suit was classy! He was purchasing it for a special sports event where jeans would be worn. I chuckle even today at this thought. Keep in mind, this was the late 70s. After leaving the Big Man's store with his new suit, we headed to get lunch. We ate hamburgers, which we could not normally afford, and had ice cream for dessert. We then headed home.

To our momentary demise, our other siblings never had

their chance of spending special time with Dad. A week later, he was feverish with infection spreading throughout his body, as shown by red spots covering his skin. It was Rocky Mountain Spotted Fever. No one had a clue about what had suddenly attacked his system. Doctors were confused. They could not detect or diagnose the illness that had consumed his body. I was eleven years old and describing it as a shock is an understatement of what I felt.

A day never went by without hearing dad's voice, seeing his smiling face, and witnessing his zeal for Christ and people. The invasion of this illness in his body came from an American dog that was tick infested with RMSF. It was unheard of and disconcerting. Dad's high-spirited and sanguine personality had suddenly left the confines of our home forever. Delirium had given him an unrecognizable personality, and this was quite confusing for all of us.

As he sat in his favorite chair, and was being examined by a doctor friend, I looked him straight in the eyes and he looked at me with confusion. He was trying to make sense of the scene because he did not recognize me or anyone else for that matter. Without any notice, he was suddenly rushed to the hospital and never returned home.

Without any notice, he was suddenly rushed to the hospital and never returned home.

Mom was at the hospital daily. She was calm and thoughtfully praying. However, I am sure her heart was shaken by this trying and difficult time. The undercurrents of life had hit our home. People were praying for Dad everywhere, yet God saw fit to take him to his eternal home. Dad's heart had been eternally shaped by God in pursuit of heaven. Therefore, his purpose was clear, and transition sweet. To be kept by God is to remember, "For if we live, we live to the Lord; and if we die, we die to the Lord. Therefore, whether we live or die, we are the Lord's" (Rom. 14:8). Even with this spiritual knowledge, Dad's death was bothersome and bittersweet for us because he was still young and thriving for Jesus, at just thirty-eight years old.

After his death, our home was somber, quiet, and without many words. People came and had gone, and my mother was left with responsibilities beyond her years. Her heart was tested and challenged to draw closer to Jesus, and that is what she did. She was convinced to move beyond her fears, worry, depression, and confusion. She desired to live in a different environment, and six months later, we moved from the parsonage into a beautiful home.

Dad's heart had been eternally shaped by God…Therefore, his purpose was clear, and transition sweet.

Prior to leaving the parsonage, and shortly after my dad's death, the Holy Spirit convinced me of my need for salvation through God's love and Christ's redemption. He used my mother to share and explain John 3:16 and to help me to personalize it. To know that I could see my father again, and spend eternity with Jesus, was life changing. At times, life was still difficult, but I believed in God's promise that He would never leave nor forsake me. Did I struggle at times with brokenness of heart? Absolutely! Although I did not know everything about Jesus when I accepted Him as Savior, I knew he lived within my heart.

The phenomenal foundation our parents provided enabled us to learn that our lives mattered. Salvation in Jesus

Christ alone would prove to be a firm foundation throughout our lives, no matter what our experiences. Their lives taught that life is meaningless without Him, but purposeful with Him because of his grace. Through Christ, we are given a new perspective and hope. In my life, God has proven to be a father to the fatherless, revealing His heart in every life-changing moment. I will share more about my testimony of faith throughout *Heart Management.*

I was married in my late twenties, and mom died several months before my wedding. I went through a church split, which was excruciating, four years later, moved to Texas, and my dear godmother, grandmother, youngest sister, and very best friend had all gone home to be with Jesus. Yes, I praise God that they are all with Him. However, another change of heart was happening in me.

Salvation in Jesus Christ alone would prove to be a firm foundation throughout our lives…

God has met and kept me in the darkest and most broken moments of my life. He will do the same for you. Life can be confusing, and we can be bound by our lack of trust in others, but God is faithful to display His good pleasures throughout our lives. So, learning to trust His process is surely rewarding.

I will never forget an older cousin who asked me how she could pray for my future endeavors. I replied by saying that I wanted to go to college. As I spoke, I was uncertain of this goal, because I had already tried it, and thought that maybe college was not for me. However, I knew that the Lord was with me, and if this desire was in His plan, He would bless it. Ironically, I enrolled in college shortly after moving to Texas. With life transitions, I pursued it intentionally, but I must tell you, this experience has not been an easy feat. My schooling has been a journey, but there have been many benefits in the process.

Life can be confusing, ...but God is faithful to display His good pleasures in us.

Through my academic years, I have learned that life is to be displayed for God's glory, while sharing it with others. When I think of my life, I count my blessings, sorrows, and the joy I have in knowing Christ. The moments of depression, loss, grief, disappointments, fainting spells, dehydration, mineral deficiencies, "spoiled dog" nightly sleep disruptions, and any lingering deficiency have been used by God tremendously. I cannot tell it all!

In every situation, a heart check is necessary. Therefore, I continue to ask the Lord to "Create in me a clean heart and renew His steadfast Spirit within me" (Ps. 51:10). I also ask myself, what is God's purpose in this period of my life? What is He trying to teach me? How can I help others with what I have been given? Proverbs 3:5-6 remind us to "Trust God's providence with all our heart, and not to lean to our own understanding, but acknowledge His existence in our lives, and He will continue to guide us into His will" (paraphrased). James 4:8 tells us to draw near to God, and He will draw nearer to us. You haven't really lived life until you are consistently being led by God's Spirit. Having God to search our heart is a lifetime partaking, because He can expose what is in there, that is, if we are interested. It was not until years later when I was facilitating a church support group that I learned my heart was still aching in various areas. A Christian counselor explained to me that I had unresolved childhood trauma that stood still in my heart. "How can trauma sit still in one's heart for so long?" I thought. She stated, "it does not mean that God cannot use a person, but His ultimate plan is to help His children completely rely on Him." He does this for every believer in Christ. Keep in mind, the sanctification process goes on until we leave this life and enter our heavenly home. When any kind of trauma remains in one's heart, his or her belief in God is limited. Therefore, your purpose is skewed. The mind creates blind spots, and your heart seeks safety.

So, what wounds are you carrying in your heart? Have you asked the Lord? Remember that nothing is hidden from Him. A wounded heart deepens open wounds and makes us feel unprotected. The enemy of our soul uses these wounds to allow others to rub alcohol in those painful areas and deepen the wounds, when left unchecked. Also, when we are not fully aware of God's enduring love, we miss out on many opportunities presented to us.

How can trauma sit still in one's heart for so long?

I love this quote by Maya Angelou, "You may not control all the events that happen to you, but you can decide not to be reduced by them." Jesus said that he came so that we may experience an abundant life (John 10:10). To experience the abundant life, Jesus desires that we take as much interest in his life so that our lives will reflect him and the power of the Holy Spirit. This point is optimal! Taking ownership of one's life is like finding precious gold. We are not defined by our circumstances, meaning, it is not what happens to you or what you have done. Ownership is revealed when your life and other people's lives are changed because of your transparency and perseverance. Is your life dramatically changing because you have opened your heart completely to the Lord? We must walk in wisdom and do whatever it takes to deal with the unresolved conflict in our hearts. God's desire for us is to have an authentic, healthy heart. Heart management begins with honesty in the heart.

Taking ownership of one's life is like finding precious gold. Ownership is revealed when your life and other people's lives are changed because of your transparency and perseverance. Is your life dramatically changing because you have opened your heart completely to the Lord?

"But let each one examine his own work, and then he will have rejoicing in himself alone, and not in another" (Gal. 6:4).

Chapter Two

AUTHENTIC HEARTS

While reading an article in the *Reader's Digest* I learned about people who were intrigued by tattoos earlier in life, but as they aged, they gained a different perspective and became disgusted by the ink that covered their body. Several of these people proactively made a conscious decision to remove their tattoos. Although painful and expensive, they did whatever was necessary to live in peace and harmony with their new perspective in life.

Others furthered their experience by deciding to turn their defeat into reward by working for a company that offers tattoo removal. They personally gained the reward of empathizing and walking through physical and emotional pain with those who were in the same predicament as in their past. These workers additionally received a huge discount to remove their own tattoos.

"A heart aligned with God is a life aligned with purpose."

Yet, others used their tattoos as a sign of remembrance for the change that had occurred within their hearts. They used their body paint as a testimony of faith to God's glory. As human beings, we are born with defective hearts. Therefore, we do things that seem right at the time, but as we mature, we understand life differently and move with a better purpose in mind. Please do not think that I am stating that tattoos are wrong and against God's will. Let your conscience be your guide. However, when we understand God's purpose in our lives, we open our hearts to Him for change. It does not matter what changes need to occur, the point is that no matter where you are in life, every human being has a need for change. Keep in mind, we have freedom in every decision. The choice is ours. We can allow our hearts to restrict and deceive us as Adam and Eve succumb to in their pride. Or, we can open our hearts to God's way and be strengthened by faith and purpose.

The truth is that we are people with huge hearts, but our hearts are tainted by this sinful world.

I'm reminded of a story that I read about a dear person's life who was a friend of my parents. He is deceased now, but in a memoir of his life, he writes about a fear that he had carried as a child into adulthood for many years. He speaks about the huge demographic shift that had taken place during Eisenhower's presidency when the interstate highway system was being built throughout America. In Chicago, where he lived, 350,000 families were displaced, and his family and other families were between a rock and a hard place. He spoke about his family living homeless for two years and during these years, kids would ignite fires and watch them burn. It was traumatic for him and his siblings to sleep at night because of the fears produced by the threat of the fires surrounding them.

He goes on to mention a dream he had for many years about a bear that would come and put him under the coffee table in the living room. He said that he had no idea what had triggered that dream for a matter of forty years. When our hearts are pure before the Lord, he will fulfill our upmost desires. This man desired change, and his change was about to come. He was watching a television program with his wife about family homelessness when an eleven-year-old girl was being interviewed. The interviewer asked the girl about her worst fear. She stated that during her homeless periods the worst fear she had was when she heard the sirens in the night. "It was the sirens in the night!" she replied. Her response triggered a response in the heart of this pastor, and he realized at that moment why he had the dreams. It was the sirens in the night that brought about the fears he had faced for over forty years.

When our hearts are pure before the Lord, He will fulfill our upmost desires.

After this realization, he had never had that dream again. His response provoked him to ask his brothers if they had remembered the sirens in the night, and both immediately cried. He asked, why hadn't they ever discussed their fears, but had kept them inside for so many years. God can use anyone to expose the truth within our hearts. He can use an eleven-year-old or a person well into their eighties. However, we must be honest and embrace what He has revealed, so that we can be effective witnesses of faith and healing.

The truth is that we are people with huge hearts, but our hearts are tainted by this sinful world. Because of Christ, God uses our brokenness as a conduit of furthering our faith and witness to others who are in need.

This man did not decide to hold on to his eye-opening revelation of the dream he endured, but decided to take the necessary steps to provide healing for his brothers by asking them about their feelings. In addition, he helped save many other lives because his life was enraptured by the power of the Holy Spirit. He was not selfish with his life, as Jesus was not selfish with his life. What will it take for you to be honest with your feelings by confronting anything the Lord brings to your attention? "Now to Him who is able to do exceedingly abundantly above all that we ask or think…" (Eph. 3:20). Amen!

An aching heart is what all human beings experience. We cannot change our hearts, but Jesus can. I want to be more like Jesus! How about you? "But without faith it is impossible to please Him, for he who comes to God must believe that He is, and that He is a rewarder of those who diligently seek Him" (Heb. 11:6).

Heart management begins with honesty of heart.

Heart management begins with honesty of heart.

STOP and check the temperature of your heart?

- Have you asked God to search your heart?
- Is your heart aligned with God's will for your life?
- What are ways that you can help someone else declutter their heart?

There is always room to Declutter!

Chapter Three

DECLUTTER YOUR HEART, DECLUTTER YOUR LIFE

Life Tips

"*Clutter is Not just the stuff on your floor; it's anything that stands between you and the life you want to be living.*"

Have you ever watched an episode of the television show called "Hoarders," where people have lived their lives in seclusion and without any accountability? Adult children are stressed to their breaking point by the mental and emotional opposition they have faced from their parents' resistance to change. Bound by their cluttered environment, and because time has lapsed, it seems that their brokenness has left them in a disillusive, depleted, and misguided state.

I am reminded of clutter in the heart when I think of how one episode in a person's life can lead to many episodes of clutter, which overtime can lead to complete destruction. The clutter we hold in our hearts is not momentary; it can lead to physical, emotional, mental, and spiritual decline. If left unaddressed, it leads to physical death. Proverbs 14:12 reminds us that, "There is a way *that seems* right to a man, but its end *is* the way of death." Do not be fooled by what you feel; feelings are unpredictable, but the longer they are extended, the shorter your life. People believe they are exempt from heart management because they trust in God and move along productively. You have heard them say,

"Give it to Jesus!" "Move on, God is with you!" Yes, Scripture is clear to give our concerns to the Lord, because God is with us. However, sometimes these are cute clichés that passively keep one in bondage from having a change of heart. Don't get me wrong, there is no other way to live without Jesus. He makes life possible, and without him, our strength fails. The hope he brings to our life allows us to endure any hardship. At the same time, Jesus bore the cross. It was the most difficult death that anyone could endure, and he was innocent. His humanity reminds us that we are broken people with broken hearts in need of God's grace and steadfast love.

The Bible says that Jesus, our great high priest, sympathizes with our weaknesses because he dealt with issues that we could not have conquered. We draw from his life because He has conquered sin, death, and the grave. However, in the process of life, God desires for us to be honest with Him by taking inventory and responsibility of our lives. These actions are what is meant as heart management. He is aware of our brokenness and desire to fill us with His peace. Our vulnerability with Him is cathartic, releasing toxicity from our souls, and moves us closer to righteous living.

Decluttering is essential for life, because it involves being pressed to the core to reveal our continual need of God's love and our dependence on Him. Scripture tells us to "pursue peace and holiness, as God himself is holy" (Heb. 12:14). Have you been pressed to the core? Have you felt as if you were drowning and could not come up for air? If we are truthful, everyone has struggles within their heart. So, we must declutter, knowing that God is on our side.

A woman in Scripture named Hannah, realized her need for the Lord as she prayed and cried out day and night for a male child. She was distraught and had an enemy that would press her to the core of her being. Did God hear her voice and the pain in her heart? He sure did, but in the process, she experienced various emotions such as long suffering, fear, rejection, bitter roots, worry, boundaries, balance, solitude, brokenness, change, and more (1 Sam. 1-3). She faced turmoil in the process of her deliverance, and God saw her brokenness and met her where she was, answered her prayer, and gave her victory by giving her a male child, named Samuel. She kept her promise to the Lord, and in return and worship, she left Samuel at the temple with Eli, the priest, to be groomed in God's complete love and call on his life.

King David also had struggles within the heart. He was as verbal, as verbal gets! In the Psalms, we see the depths of David's soul as he wrestles with managing his heart. We attribute the heart as the soul of the person, and David expressed his entire being to the Lord. The Bible says that he was a man after God's own heart because of his authenticity, transparency, and vulnerability.

Why would God attribute His character to a broken man like David? David had no qualms about calling on the name of the Lord. He cried out intentionally to the Lord to answer all his woes. Why does God allow us to observe King David's life in the book of Psalms? Today, we would say that David must be oppressed with the psychological disorder, Bipolar.

Have you thought about the inconsistencies in your life? God was with David. He answered his prayers. There are times when He answered yes, no, and wait. David prayed that God would search his heart so that godless ideologies would be exposed for repentance. David prayed to God to destroy his enemies. David prayed that he would have a pure heart. David prayed for his illegitimate child to live although he was born from an adulterous affair. David prayed about everything.

David not only prayed, but he also worshipped the Lord to the point where his clothing was falling off. Ha! Are you willing to embarrass yourself in the flesh for Jesus? David would most likely say, I was not embarrassed, but rather, in awe of my God. In the fullness of his heart, David desired to model God's character. Is there any question, now, why God said he was a man after His own heart? Are you a man or woman after God's own heart? Read the book of Psalms and find your place of discomfort in need of fulfillment. The bottom line is that real people need Jesus, and God answers prayer! As I reflect on my grandfather's life, he would sing a song called, "You've Got to Pray!" He meant every word because he knew how to pray and get an answer from the Lord.

Jesus, the perfect Lamb of God thought it not selfish to die for sinful and helpless humanity. He rose from the grave and lives forevermore! He didn't have to do it, but I'm so glad he did! He is our Redeemer, Rescuer, and provides respite for our weary souls. One day, we will see him face to face where every eye shall behold him, and those who have trusted in him, by faith, will be made perfectly whole. Do you trust him with your life?

"If You Declutter Your Heart,
You will Declutter Your Life."

TIP ONE: SELF-REFLECTION

"Examine yourselves, whether ye be in the faith; prove your own selves" (2 Cor. 1:5).

"The three habits of the heart that nurture a reflective life are reading the moment, reflecting on the moment, and responding to the moment." Self-reflection takes time for introspection. It does not rush the process, but takes in the past, present, and what could become of the future. "Life throws all of us curveballs, and it can take time and reflection to figure out how to move forward afterward." During the late eighties, I met many friends from across the country as I first entered college. I was twenty-one and had joined the basketball team, which was an unfulfilled goal I had desired in high school. Fearful and intimidated by the environment, I pressed forward. However, I struggled academically and in faith. I studied accounting and attended school for one year but found myself returning home believing college was not for me.

After reflecting and regrouping, my best friend and I decided to attend a technical school and studied data entry and word processing. We graduated and worked for Mellon Bank in downtown Philadelphia. I worked long hours to earn extra money. However, I struggled with the idea of purpose. I thought, "Where am I going in life?" My heart was unsettled, shaken, and as I reflected on my life, I was afraid.

The Lord took me back to the time when I first accepted His love. As I mentioned earlier, when I was eleven years old, my dad had gone home to be with Jesus. During this period of grief, I thought, "Why would God take a loving man to heaven so abruptly?!" Yes, life was cooperative under the authority and care of the Almighty, but in my young mind, it was confusing.

I reflected on my life at a church revival when I was just seven years old. In the 70s, Baptist churches would mimic the Great Awakening period of the 1700s. These churches would bring in evangelists who were fired up, and ready to preach the gospel of Jesus Christ to motivate people toward faith. Everyone looked forward to these revivals because they were uplifting, emotional, and distinct from the typical church service.

In our church revival, Evangelist Ernie Wilson came to preach for an amazing one week. People were saved, and lives were changed. I remember sitting in my seat enraptured by the emotion, music, and praise. However, I did not consider faith. There was no prompting by the Holy Spirit, and no heartfelt change, but when the invitation to Christ was given, I decided to walk to the front of the church. I smiled, everyone clapped, but my faith was insincere. Years later, I wondered how many hearts had not been truly changed but walked, as I had walked, down the aisle.

After the Lord had taken dad home, death became a reality to me for anyone, at any time, and any place. My heart was filled with sorrow. Weighed down by insomniac nights, God's Spirit brought to my attention my need for salvation. He had revealed my impure motives for walking up front at the revival. With this reality, I ran into my mother's bedroom with tears in my eyes. My heart was full of fear, and I shared my feelings concerning my dad's death and my eternal destiny. Empty, broken, and confused, I bowed my head and closed my eyes as my mother led me to the Lord Jesus Christ through John 3:16. I repented of my sins and accepted God's grace through Jesus' sacrifice at Calvary. I believed that either I would go to see him as my Savior, or that he would return for me someday. That experience was a turning point in my life. I was saved and would one day see my father again. I did not understand everything I needed to know about Jesus, but I knew I could trust His promises. John 10:28 says, "And I give them eternal life, and they shall never perish; neither shall anyone snatch them out of My hand." I was sure of my salvation and since that time, God has shown His mighty hand in my life.

Self-reflection is essential. It allows one to observe and reflect on how far we have come and the needs we desperately have for God. It reveals the sin in our heart, but the reward of God's grace. It serves the purpose of renewal, strengthening, remembering, and weighing our emotions, thoughts, and experiences. It helps us to face our fears and sorrows, and motivates us to move with passion, peace, forgiveness, freedom, and joy. If we correctly and objectively understand our faith journey, we can progress into new heights and be strengthened with integrity, dignity, and purpose.

Journaling, another form of self-reflection: Journaling allows us to take an in-depth, responsible look at our feelings. It helps us put our thoughts and feelings on paper to process our past and present needs and future steps. It allows for descriptive writing and considerable change. If we cannot take the time to check our internal thermostat emotionally, we will die. Emotional death can lead to physical death because our bodies were not meant to live in carnality (Rom. 8:6). We are hope-centered people. Our attitude and conduct must be aligned with Christ's character (Phil. 2:5). "Reflecting on the moment is engaging our mind to see what's beneath the surface." Journaling helps us, by God's Spirit, to confront limiting beliefs and blind spots, and allows us to recognize God's providential care.

***Prayer, the most essential form of self-reflection*:** Prayer takes us to higher levels beyond ourselves because we seek dependence on our Creator. It reminds us that God is sovereign and sensitive to our depraved condition and will respond accordingly. You can save your life by seeking His wisdom.

George Muller was a charismatic guy who prayed about everything. In particular, he prayed for the needs of children in an orphanage. Although many of his prayers were spontaneous, God responded almost immediately because of the sincerity of his heart. You can read more about his life in the orphanage through his biography. Our relationship with God reflects our need for His provisions, but we must continually acknowledge His presence and capability to supply all our needs. "And my God shall supply all your need according to His riches in glory by Christ Jesus" (Phil. 4:19).

Self-reflection begins with you. No one can take responsibility for how God is speaking to you.

CONSIDER:

In what ways are you reflecting on your life?
Simply write down three emotions, thoughts, and/or experiences.

1.
2.
3.

Are you trusting the Creator with your life?
How is He speaking to you right now?
Consider: Ps. 139:13-16.

1.
2.
3.

"I believe that doubts, honestly expressed and wrestled with, produce a faith that is stronger and more intimate than doubts suppressed under the veneer of faith."

JOURNAL #1

Are you taking an honest look within?
Write about a specific turning point in your life?

TIP TWO: EXPRESS YOURSELF

"There is a time to listen for understanding and a time to speak" (Eccl. 3:7).

I had taken on a supervisory role within a residential treatment setting, and I was challenged to speak the truth in love for healing and change. I was six months into this role, and the children's brokenness, due to their past circumstances, was heartbreaking and difficult to witness. They expressed their feelings through outbursts of anger, verbal abuse, and physical fighting. Brief therapeutic intervention training was provided for the staff, but several workers struggled to properly support these children. Rather than jumping straight to the physical aspects of therapeutic intervention, the children needed us to patiently listen to them. They needed time, respect, security, and respite for their souls.

In their book, Caring Assertiveness, authors Haugk, Bretscher, and Musser states,

> Assertiveness involves respecting both the person you're relating to and yourself, so no matter how intense your feelings may be, treat the other person with respect. Doing so keeps the lines of communication open and makes it more likely that your message will have the intended effect. On the other hand, labeling the person, name-calling, making sarcastic remarks, or otherwise putting them down will probably inflame the situation or shut down communication.

I expressed the need for further training and brainstorming ideas to create a more trusting environment. After these new steps were initiated, as the children experienced patience and understanding from the staff, their attitude, conduct, and communication changed. These new steps, initiated by the staff, not only changed the children but also the staff who implemented them.

Trying new steps to create new patterns within the environment was difficult and daunting. Through consistency, the more we allowed them to express their feelings responsibly, the environment became trusting and productive.

Healing occurs as we empty ourselves to the Lord. Our friendships and communities are changed because of our voices. Just as we opened our hearts to listen to the hearts of the children in the residential treatment setting, God opens His sensitive ears to our voices, and we find warmth and comfort in Him. "I love the Lord, because He has heard my voice and my supplications. Because He has inclined His ear to me, therefore I will call upon Him as long as I live" (Ps. 116:1-2).

As we talk with God about our concerns and confusion, He gives us clarity and reminds us of His faithfulness and enduring love. We should walk in step with the Spirit so that our voices might cultivate understanding, offer encouragement, inspire others, and provide support. Increased strength and change come through an open heart and awareness of God and ourselves.

CONSIDER:

- ✓ How are you seeking the Spirit to impact someone's life?
- ✓ In what way have others used their voice to impact your walk with God?

"The only way to find your voice is to use it."

JOURNAL #2

Is there a person that comes to mind who you can provide listening with understanding?

How will you be intentional in spending time with this person?

TIP THREE: FORGIVE

"And be kind to one another, tenderhearted, forgiving one another, even as God in Christ forgave you" (Eph. 4:32).

After nineteen years spent in prison for stealing a piece of bread to feed his hungry family, Jean Valjean had developed hate for the society he had lived in. He became a vagabond and lived as a thief. That is, until he experienced profound redemption and grace from the bishop of a monastery. Check out the book, *Le Miserable*, by Victor Hugo. God has a way of turning our defeat into His good.

I have been tested in more ways than one to forgive, and most likely, you have been, too. It is not an easy task to forgive those who have harmed you. However, when I think about the people, I have disappointed, whether intentionally or unintentionally, I'm humbled by God's grace.

In Matthew 18:21, Peter asked Jesus how many times he should forgive a brother who has sinned against him. In asking this question, Peter had already considered the answer, but it was limited. The numerical amount Peter specified, "up to seven times," was considered most kind and humble, according to Jewish custom. "Peter thought that he was generous, as the Jewish rule was three times (Amos 1:6). "The man who asks such a question does not really know what forgiveness means" (Plummer)." His question goes back to verse 15. 'Against me' is genuine here." Peter's focus was on himself, not others. His defense was not God-honoring and for the perfecting of the church.

How many times have you been offended by the same person, and because of their consistent pattern, you keep a ledger of the many times they have offended you? Even when we are offended, we must take our eyes off self and please the Lord with our actions.

The Spirit of God has had me perform extreme heart management when I have been most hurt and offended by another who has habitually harmed me. Somehow, He redirects my focus and convinces me that it is not my job to cleanse the person of their ill wills against me. It is His job. I'm led to release my hands from their neck, pray, and trust the matter to God.

When we keep a record of the many offenses a person has committed against us, we prove our ignorance in the matter of forgiveness. Jesus redirected Peter back to God's character and lofty thoughts. He answers Peter's question according to God's wisdom, "not seven times, Peter, but 'seventy times seven." Believers are held accountable to God's standard as Jesus is the ultimate model of forgiveness. Therefore, forgiveness is not an option; it is a command. Without it, God holds us responsible for our unforgiving hearts, and we limit His blessings in our lives.

Forgiveness is essential for spiritual health and vitality. It does not mean that we must befriend or accept someone's toxic behavior or projected harm. God has the final say in those matters (Rom. 12:19). "While God requires me to unconditionally forgive the business partner who cheats me, he does not require that I remain in business with him. I can forgive someone without being reunited with that person." Forgiveness continues to set boundaries even in our relationships. It is not complicated. It seeks God's highest good.

Forgiveness also releases us from the torment of self-judgment and of judging others. Why enter a bitter state and risk your well-being? Is it worth it? Matthew 5:44 says, "But I say to you, love your enemies, bless those who curse you, do good to those who hate you, and pray for those who spitefully use you and persecute you…" When we forgive, God is glorified, and He deserves our entire hearts.

Last, we forget that we have a choice in how we clear our hearts toward others. We can just trust the Lord with the situation. Or we can confront the person at the right time, and as God leads. In doing either of these, you will experience God's peace (Matt. 5:23-24). There is a higher calling waiting that you have not yet seen when you release the unforgiveness in your heart and forgive anyone who has sinned against you (Phil. 3:14).

CONSIDER:

- ✓ Are you holding on to unforgiveness?
- ✓ In what way do you need to forgive someone who has disappointed you?

The past can be a kill-joy if you hold on to the things you cannot control. On the other hand, "The past is your ally in repairing your present and ensuring a better future."

JOURNAL #3

Write down what is holding you back from releasing yourself from the grip of unforgiveness?

What is God's will in the context of forgiveness (Matt. 5:23–24)?

How will you do whatever is necessary to respond to God's will?

TIP FOUR: PRACTICE GRATITUDE

"In everything give thanks; for this is the will of God in Christ Jesus for you" (I Thess. 5:18).

His name was Robert Scheller, and he was the owner of a company called Pretest Excel. He was brilliant, yet humble. He, his wife, and their children lived in a mansion and by worldly standards, had all life could offer. His wife was a lawyer, and they had a housekeeper, but they needed someone to take care of their children. I worked for a company named Special Care, which was an organization that aided taking care of family members in the home. I was assigned Bob's home and had become comfortable with his family. On many occasions, I saw bulk mail continuously coming and going from the home. I was curious and asked about his occupation and the ongoing mail I noticed. Additionally, I offered to do administrative work, if needed. Bob hired me as his administrative assistant. I organized the bulk mailings, brought in staff to assist, answered phone calls, organized books and office supplies, completed banking, traveled, and whatever else needed to be done.

With each opportunity given, I shared my faith with Bob, and even some of his peers, but I'm not sure if he ever came to faith. As I mentioned earlier, Bob seemed to have it all together by worldly standards, but what I know for sure is that Jesus' involvement in our lives fulfills us. Bob was a man of integrity, good values and had a good reputation. However, years later, he and his wife divorced, and I learned that he had passed away from cancer in 2009. After learning about his death, I said a brief prayer, thanking the Lord for allowing this man to have had such a profound impact in my life.

Gratitude is like a blazing fire that decimates weeds. “Giving thanks always for all things to God the Father in the name of our Lord Jesus, Christ” (Ephesians 5:20). Bob had human problems, but he maintained focus on serving others and appreciating life.

CONSIDER:

- ✓ What are you grateful for?
- ✓ Who has impacted your life?
- ✓ If they are still living, consider writing them a letter of appreciation. Let them know how they have impacted your life. Or just call them.

"As we express our gratitude, we must never forget that the highest appreciation is not to utter words, but to live by them."

JOURNAL #4

Do you have a home, food, and clothing? Are your lights turned on? Do you have hot water? Do you have gas, electricity, or both? Do you have transportation? Do you have special friendships? Who is that special someone that has impacted your life? Write down your appreciation for these necessities, and/or this person.

TIP FIVE: SET BOUNDARIES

"The heart is deceitful above all things, and desperately wicked; Who can know it" (Jer. 17:9)?

My son was just six years old when a troubled young boy his age, in a homeschool co-op, had chosen to take out his anger on him. Anger consumed this little guy's demeanor, and he impulsively stabbed my son with a pencil near his eye. I was upset, but the Lord calmed my heart, and I regained control over my feelings. I prayed for the young boy, even though it was a traumatic experience for my son.

This incident opened candid conversations with my children about boundaries in relationships and the desperation one feels in the heart when needs go unmet. We talked about healthy and unhealthy boundaries in our friendships. The Lord wanted to reveal, through this child's patterns, that sin pervades the human heart from birth.

David said, "Behold, I was brought forth in iniquity, and in sin my mother conceived me" (Ps. 51:5). Another teaching point was that God's protection is present in our lives, and that He can change broken hearts and use all of us for His glory, honor, and praise. We talked about how, as believers, we must always pray for people and be witnesses (I Thess. 5:17), but that it is okay to set boundaries and be balanced in our thinking.

When our children endure hardship over the enemy's schemes, it is difficult to see them fight through adversity. However, God uses our handling of crisis as a testimony of faith and promise. In any case, boundaries are essential for living a balanced life.

Cloud and Townsend writes:

> The problem is that sometimes you see boundaries as an offensive weapon. Nothing could be further from the truth. Boundaries are a defensive tool. Appropriate boundaries don't control, attack, or hurt anyone. They simply prevent your treasures from being taken at the wrong time.

Wisdom is another lesson we learn through maintaining boundaries. In God's love we have choices. We don't have to settle for anything in the process of pointing people to Jesus Christ. We must value our lives and express mutual respect for others when boundaries are set. Discernment is key to distinguish between the good, bad, and ugly.

Boundaries pertaining to time must also be set to accomplish anything in life. Whether it is people, places, or things, we must stick to our convictions to be authentic and productive. "Even when someone has a valid problem, and there are times when we can't sacrifice for some reason or another." We cannot respond to every need others have. Therefore, we must pray for the person and know that God will work the situation out for their good.

Keep in mind that Jesus set boundaries on many occasions, like when he left the multitude to be alone with the Father (Matt. 14:22-23). In building our relationships, we must depend on the Lord and teach others to do the same. We must set limits and use our time wisely. People may or may not disagree with us, but "true intimacy is only built around the freedom to disagree." With that said, we have the freedom to respond wisely and gladly disagree. Do you agree?

CONSIDER:

- ✓ How have you set boundaries?
- ✓ Are you having ongoing conversations with your children regarding boundaries?
- ✓ Are you sticking to your convictions?

"One of the first signs that you're beginning to develop boundaries is a sense of resentment, frustration, or anger at the subtle and not-so-subtle violations in your life. Just as radar signals the approach of a foreign missile, your anger can alert you to boundary violations in your life"

JOURNAL #5

Are you establishing boundaries in your relationships? If so, write them down. If not, what boundaries can you establish today?

TIP SIX: SELF-CARE

"Beloved, I pray that you may prosper in all things and be in health, just as your soul prospers" (3 John 1:2).

When you face any kind of opposition or difficulty, self-care is essential to your life. How can one love and understand God's will if he or she is not physically and emotionally taking good care of himself or herself? We reflect God's providential care when we consider ourselves in the process of our witness. Matthew 22:39 reminds us to love others as we love ourselves. If we are not taking good care of ourselves, we cannot love others as Jesus instructed.

When God created the seventh day, it was for rest. He also created stress hormones to warn us of our need for a personal time-out. Colbert asks, "Have you ever wondered why certain people just can't seem to relax–they are wound up over some problem or issue on a nearly constant basis?" He answers, "The reason may very well be that the person has lived at a heightened state of emotion for so long that he or she has become addicted to stress hormones." Many people have driven themselves to illness because they have refused to pay attention to the warning signs in their body.

As much as Jesus loved his disciples, there were numerous times when he took time away to rest, reset, and talk with the Father. When Satan tempted him in the wilderness, after fasting for forty days and nights, I'm sure his cortisol levels were raised, but what did he do? He used the Word of God as a weapon against the world, the flesh, and the devil, reminding Satan of his Creator. After the devil left Jesus, God sent ministering angels to care for him.

Once in a homeschool co-op, I had been tested to the core, and I remembered praying daily that God would save these people because they were totally different from where I had come from. God seemed to chuckle, and I continued to be tested. I was already dealing with a bit of depression, based on the disappointments and changes in life. However, it wasn't the people or my circumstances that God needed me to understand. He wanted me to experience trusting Him amid these circumstances and refresh myself with His tender loving care (Eph. 3).

"There are moments in life when there is nothing you can do to control what is happening. In those times, find your hiding place under the shelter of God's wings." God's wings cover us even when we can't utter the right words in prayer. God's wings go before us even when we are quoting His uncompromising Word. As we mature in life and faith, we realize the importance of taking care of ourselves spiritually, physically, emotionally, and mentally. We become more aware of our needs, what can harm us, and what we must avoid or face head-on (1 Cor. 14:20; 2 Pet. 3:18). These actions allow us to put off uncertainty and replace old attitudes, beliefs, and behaviors with a sense of new beginnings.

Most importantly, spiritually, we return to the basic principles of faith such as reading, praying, meditating, and studying God's Word. Socially, we gain support through like-minded communities. Physically, we choose exercise, nutritional changes, and even a back massage would relieve us of the stress we feel. Emotionally, we combat negative feelings by replacing them with truth and counsel. We may need to maintain boundaries with those who cause us direct or indirect emotional harm. Mentally, we "take our thoughts captive and make them obedient to Christ" (2 Cor. 10:5). If needed, we may need therapeutic counsel for clear mental and emotional processing. Whatever the case, God's desire is that we do whatever is necessary to become proactive stewards of our lives.

Self-care begins with an awareness of our Creator. He created us in His image, and we must not compromise our health. We must do what it takes to guard our hearts and our minds in Christ Jesus (Phil. 4:6-8). Self-care is not selfish. It is required for awareness, ownership, and to impact someone else's life. It allows us to be present and productive wherever we go (Matt. 22:36-37).

CONSIDER:

- ✓ When life is disappointing where can we run for strength and refreshment?
- ✓ Read Psalms 46.
- ✓ Are you spending time with God?
- ✓ Are you prayerful? Are you getting the rest you need?
- ✓ Are you choosing joy? Are you exercising and eating nutritiously?
- ✓ Are you replacing your negative thoughts with God's Word?
- ✓ Are you seeking support in supportive environments?

"You are more precious than jewels" (Prov. 31:10).

JOURNAL #6

David prayed, "Search me, oh God, and know my heart, try me, and know my anxieties; and see if there is any wicked way in me, and lead me in the way of everlasting" (Ps. 139:23-24).

In what ways are you taking inventory of your life?
Has God revealed the conditions of your heart?
How is He speaking to you?

TIP SEVEN: SEEK SUPPORT

"Though one may be overpowered by another, two can withstand him. And a threefold cord is not quickly broken" (Eccl. 4:12).

The Discovery Channel was one of our favorite channels to watch throughout our children's homeschooling experience. The animal kingdom was the object lesson in their learning about God's provision, protection, and providential care. There were times when we watched an isolated animal from the deer family fall prey to the predatory "pride" family. These lions were fierce in providing food for their family. As hunting season began, they would carefully observe their prey with patience, rest in the grass while watching from a distance, track with their eyes, listen intently with their ears, and relax their muscles in readiness to steal their prey. As they slowly but smoothly head toward the deer, they would suddenly burst into motion, sprinting at explosive speed toward the deer that has fallen behind the herd. The lion takes it down with its paw to knock it off balance, and clamps its teeth into the deer's neck, suffocating it, and the feeding begins.

Human beings are like deer, in that, isolation is the enemy's territory. If he can make you discount your purpose and walk through life alone, he will win the battle through your fears and disappointments and lead you to the lions. Ecclesiastes 4:12 tells us, "Though one may be overpowered by another, two can withstand him. And a threefold cord is not quickly broken." Community is necessary for growth and development. It helps one maintain balance in life and have the accountability needed for protection, wisdom, and productivity.

Support is essential, no matter what we experience or where we find ourselves in life. Those who deprive themselves of support will only go as far as their choices take them. The Bible says that one should not be a hermit, because God created humanity with others in mind. He would not have created Eve if Adam were to live life alone.

Support allows one to see life from various viewpoints. Proverb 27:17 says, "*As* iron sharpens iron, so a man sharpens the countenance of his friend." There is safety in seeking accountability through a small group, a counselor, a coach, a therapist, or a spiritual director. You get the point! They will help you move with purpose if you need healing or if you are stuck in a particular area. A life group will provide community, like-minded support, and encouragement as you move forward with greater passion and purpose (Eph. 4:12; Prov. 11:14, 27:17). So never fail to take advantage of being under others' care. Be wise by never walking alone.

Supportive Networks:
Focus on the Family
Hope for the Heart Counseling
Hope in the Night Counseling
Hope Talk Podcast
New Life Live
Revive Our Hearts
Truth for Life Podcast
AACC (Association of American Christian Counselors)
Being Known Podcast with Dr. Curt Thompson

Recommended Books:
A Better Way to Think by H. Norman Wright
Boundaries by Cloud and Townsend
Co-Dependency by June Hunt
Deadly Emotions by Dr. Don Colbert
Honestly by Sheila Walsh (May be out of print)
Let Them by Mel Robbins
Seeing Yourself Through God's Eyes by June Hunt
She's Still There by Chrystal Evans Hurst
Switch On Your Brain by Dr. Caroline Leaf
The Deepest Place by Dr. Curt Thompson
The Garden Within by Dr. Anita Phillips
You Are More Than You Know by Patsy Clairmont
Building Bounce by Marcus Warner and Stefanie Hinman
Personality Assessment: Connect Assessment -
https://www.connectassessment.com/

CONSIDER:

- ✓ Are you walking alone?
- ✓ What steps are you taking to seek support?

"The Purpose in a man's heart is like deep water, but a man of understanding will draw it out" (Prov. 20:5).

JOURNAL #7

How is God speaking to you through the below Scriptures?

- ✓ Pray (1 Thess. 5:17; Phil. 4:6).
- ✓ Study to show yourself approved by God (2 Tim. 3:15; 1 Tim. 4:15).
- ✓ Meditate on Scripture (Jos.1:8; Phil. 4:8; Ps. 119:11; Rom. 12:2).
- ✓ Listen for God's voice in all matters of life (2 Pet. 1:3).

PART II
LIFE RIP CURRENTS

"There is a tide in the affairs of men, which taken at the flood, leads on to fortune; omitted, all the voyage of their life is bound in shallows and in miseries. On such a full sea we are now afloat; And we must take the current when it serves, or lose our ventures."

Chapter Four

IDENTITY IN HEART

Who Are You?

"Who are you?" "Who are…you?" "Who?" "Are." "You!"

Almost twenty-four years ago, I will never forget the day I entered my public speaking class. I was looking to make new friends and give my life further purpose in Texas. So, I returned to school. I had never taken a public speaking course, so I was a bit nervous. On the first day of class, my heart was tested when, to my surprise, the Professor asked, "Who Are You?" Insecurities began flooding my thoughts.

I thought, Why is he asking this question in a public speaking class? Is it because he wants to see how many people speak well for impromptu speeches? Is he testing our ability to formulate a truth or opinion about ourselves? Why did he ask this question? More importantly, how shall I answer it?

I tried to think quickly, but due to my brain rush and mental block, I began to get stumped about who was asking the question, why he had asked, and what my response should be. My thoughts were consumed with my own questions. Should I answer this question based on my relationship with Christ? Should I state my status as a wife, a sister, or a friend? How about my work experience? I had no children at the time. How should I respond? After all, we had no clue what he was looking for. Did he want a short answer or an explanation?

"Angela Carwheel…who are you?" He had called on me before I could thoughtfully answer the question. I felt even more stumped because I had failed to listen to my classmate's responses. I also felt selfish because I did not appreciate the value of the class camaraderie. Before I knew it, I blurted out, "I am a child of God, who…" and he cut me off. The questions in my mind persisted, but I was satisfied with my answer. However, I still had human insecurities. My answer came from my heart, and I knew the Lord was with me.

Rocky Mountain Spotted Fever is a bacterial disease spread by the bite of an infected tick, and it had been largely undetected throughout the 1970s. It was discovered in my father's body after he had died. However, while he was alive, the doctors used many treatments to figure out what had invaded his body. It was not until two years later, after his death, that the CDC produced a statement of concern regarding the spread of RMSF.

Identity plays a huge role in every human being's life. God has given us biological constructs in our DNA that allow a person to prove parental connection. In a similar way, He has placed His identity in the hearts of every man, woman, boy, and girl (Eccl. 3:11). The Bible says that we were made in the image of God; therefore, we can identify with Him as Creator, and know Him as Father, through His Son, Jesus Christ.

My dad never met his biological father, but he was able to bypass his natural genetics and cling to the God who loved him with grace and gave him life for all eternity. So, in a natural sense, it does not matter if life has not treated you well regarding your earthly father, or mother, in this matter. God has no beginning or end. He is gracious to all who will trust in Him. Jesus gives purpose, and my father knew this well. Dad's life in Christ revealed that he was everything his heavenly Father had created him to be. In this truth, he was enough.

The answer to the question my professor had asked was already in me. I just had to live a little longer to understand that everything I am, is who God designed me to be. I am loved, valued, accepted, and have been given purpose forever!

Marcus Warner's explanation of our sense of identity developed from birth to adulthood, in his book, *Breakthrough,* is phenomenal! He says,

> As babies, the part of our brains that knows who we are is largely undeveloped. This part of the brain grows through thousands of relational experiences...The brain's sense of identity is not formed by information but rather by attachment. What we believe about ourselves is important, but when it comes to identity formation there is something even deeper than our beliefs. When we learn to form joy-filled attachments and we get our beliefs anchored in our identity in Christ, we have a powerful one-two punch that makes for a very stable sense of self.

In my innermost being, I was attached to my mother and father's love, and the love they had received from their heavenly Father, through their Savior, Jesus Christ, alone. Although I did not know Christ as Savior while my dad lived, I embraced his sacrifice for my sins through my father's death and the life he had lived. The love he displayed opened the windows of my heart to see God in a totally different light.

Never falter or be shaken when you face a question such as, "Who are you?" God will remind you of His love no matter what circumstance you're in. He gave you life and will continue to reveal His identity to you as you open your heart to Him. I am reminded daily that God gives options. We can soar above life's rip currents and rely on God's perfect promises. Or we can sink and let the rip tide take us under. Knowing who we are is essential in faith and opportunity. When we soar above life uncertainties, increased faith in the only One who keeps His promises is revealed in us. Our identity in Christ holds us together in the core of our innermost being. Yes, he shows up even when we are tested. Continue to allow Him to fasten every twist and turn in life as you take refuge in Him. After all, He is our identity.

CONSIDER:

- ✓ What question regarding identity stands out in your mind?
- ✓ At your core, do you truly believe that you are enough?
- ✓ Do you see yourself through God's eyes?
- ✓ If you were asked this question, what would first come to your mind?

"In this life, we discover who we are, how we are wired, and why we exist."

JOURNAL #8

Detail below how you would answer the question, "Who Are You?"

Chapter Five

A GRIEVING HEART

Where Grief Abounds

Mourn the loss but gather the flowers.

My mother was an outstanding, gracious, meek, and unique woman of faith. I was twenty-eight years old and soon to be married when the Lord took her home from battling years of ovarian cancer. Her death was three months before my wedding date, and it was difficult to handle. I was grateful for her life, but hunger pains were left in my heart for her voice and motherly care in my life. I felt a bit short-changed. In defense, I mourned what she could not give in life, rather than applaud all the treasures that she had given to me.

In her struggle while living through cancer, I resisted her death. Devastated, I chose not to empathize with the visual and emotional exposure of her pain. I was grieving her loss, although she had not yet died.

Grief often clouds the beauty of the life that is present. It allows one to identify only a skewed version of the flowers that comprises a person's unique being. I was about to be married and felt like a whirlwind had swept my heart.

Mom's life reflected promise and purpose. She gave her children a sense of security in a peaceful home. She gave us treasures through faith and prayer. She gave us a listening ear. She was kind, gentle, generous, and joyful. She gave us a sense of community between church and family. The beauty of sharing within a Christ-centered community will increase the heart of any human being. Grief is a difficult process, but another piece of our life's puzzle. During this time, we must cling to the God of enduring promise and hope and cherish the lasting mark each person leaves behind. We can mourn the loss but never forget to gather each flower.

Mom loved her family but understood that life was short. She learned extended grace because she felt God's presence throughout her life. She was sick as a child with scoliosis, a heart condition, and anemia. Having been in and out of the hospital as a teenager, life was difficult, but as an adult, she did not complain or wear her pain. Instead, she trusted the Lord for strength, and through courage and tenacity, she learned how to manage life. Grace was present through these experiences. She understood that she was undeserving of life and lived to appreciate the time she had been given.

Mourn the loss but gather the flowers. Mom had to mourn the loss of depleted energy, fatigue, and lost sick days. However, there was still the joy of the Lord which gave her strength for each day and bright hope for tomorrow. She had to mourn what appeared to be losses and redirect her attention by appreciating her family and friends, as well as by serving others. She had to mourn the loss of her youngest sister's death, but enjoyed the memories of laughter, talking, and the differences in their personalities and walks of life.

She mourned the loss of her husband, yet, reminisced on the joy of him calling her "My-dear!" and the ongoing love he brought to our family and ministry. She had to mourn the loss of wayward children and embrace the flowers of hugs, kisses, laughter, school achievements, and their occupations to help enhance our family's living. After being diagnosed with ovarian cancer, I am sure she mourned when she realized the toll that chemo fatigue had taken on her body, the weakness, nausea, and the ill-will of the disease. She chose to replace any negative thoughts, with rejoicing in God's goodness and mercy.

Mom mourned her losses due to the impact of life trials. However, she gathered magnificent flowers as she gracefully journeyed and walked with the Lord. As Jesus suffered, she understood the reality of her suffering. As Jesus knelt before the Father, she realized her prayers could reach heaven faster than worry could sustain her grief. The grace she had given to others allowed her to live a secure, loving, and prosperous life. "You may, because of your circumstances, find that life has left you carrying an empty basket. If so, remember that it may appear empty, but actually it contains endless possibilities." Allow grief to take its course but remember to pick up the flowers in the process.

CONSIDER:

- ✓ It is okay to mourn your losses but gather each flower as you move forward. There are flowers in every aspect of our grief. It does not matter what kind of loss you experience. Each time you worry, you take away from the beauty and pleasure of each petal awaiting you.
- ✓ Are you mourning your losses, but gathering the flowers?
- ✓ Remember, grace is not only for others, but it is also for you.

"Grief is a normal response to the loss of any significant person, object, or opportunity. It is an experience of deprivation and anxiety that can show itself in one's behavior, emotions, thinking, physiology, interpersonal relationships, and spirituality."

JOURNAL #9

How are you preparing yourself to mourn your losses and gather the flowers?

Chapter Six

A CONTENTED HEART

What Have You Done?

My doctor had grown up in a Holland orphanage but became the apple of her adoptive father's eyes. Although a doctor, she felt she could never live up to her dad's standards. She dated a guy for many years to discover that marriage was not something she desired. She believed marriage was an American hope and dream, and that is it. She could not relate to the biblical definition of marriage and God's covenantal blessing of the two becoming one flesh.

The concept of a covenant relationship in marriage, where two become one flesh, is mind-bottling for most people. Even the apostle Paul refers to it as a great mystery. I wonder if my doctor struggled with the lack of parental acceptance and appreciation for the person she had become. Therefore, she resisted her parents hope of the typical American dream of marriage life with children. My life may have depicted the very thing she despised. Therefore, perhaps it was difficult for her to empathize or conceptualize our differences. Each time I had an appointment, we would always have great conversations. She would emphasize my thorough knowledge of the Bible, from her perspective, anyhow. However, she denied God's presence, and she stated she had an atheist background.

During my first appointment, she asked me, "What have you done, Angela?" Prior to raising and homeschooling our children, I worked and continued my education. At this specific time, in addition to homeschooling, I was attending a Seminary. Life was not easy, but God was present. I discussed our children's ages and our approach to life, which included homeschooling through co-ops, sports, dance, piano, drum lessons, board games, and regular conversations about life, among other things. Her question threw me off guard because I had already mentioned my husband and my decision to homeschool. I felt insulted, and my silence spoke volumes.

On the other hand, I thought to myself, why did her question make me feel so uncomfortable when that was a part of my story? Why couldn't I have viewed her question without judgment? Her question reflected her perspective in life. It was her opinion, not my reality. Her upbringing and journey influenced her prejudgments, decisions, and ideologies. At the same time, it challenged the beauty of my heavenly call. I am a mom, called by God to raise the two children He entrusted to me. I should have felt secure and confident enough to walk in God's calling without dispute. But why did I have a problem with her question? What was my standard of living? What did I value? Who was I living for?

What made me discontented with the rejection I had felt? I was offended by a worldview that differed from mine and allowed it to trigger a negative response within me. There was an unmet need I had felt, and the Lord had to reveal the attitude of my heart. After much introspection, the realization and acceptance of who God created me to be as a mother made me stronger and wiser as a person. I kept in the forefront of my brain, "He who calls you is faithful, who also will do it." (1 Thess. 5:24).

Modeling Jesus is a process (1 Pet. 1:16-17). His identity is being developed and actualized in the lives of those who are seeking him. We have nothing to fear and nothing to lose when we are doing God's will. "But godliness with contentment is great gain..." (I Tim. 6:6). Who are you living for? Are you in competition with a worldly ideology? Are you content in heart with whom God has called you to be?

CONSIDER:

✓ Have you ever experienced a similar situation as a mom or dad? My kids are older now, and I will be their forever Mom. Now that makes me happy!

"A mother is she who can take the place of all others but whose place no one else can take."

JOURNAL #10

Scripture reminds us that comparisons are unwise. Have you accepted God's call in your life? How can you be content and secure in your personal call and reject worldly comparisons?

Chapter Seven

AN INTENTIONAL HEART

No, Is Relational

The word "no," communicates boundaries, and is a form of respect for self and others. We learn to use it in our toddler years by often mimicking our parents' communication to us. During these precious years, we are curious and in a phase of discovering new things. By saying "no," our parents used protective measures to help balance our thinking and keep us out of trouble. "Even a child is known by his deeds, whether what he does *is* pure and right (Prov. 20:11). Godly parents provide spiritual direction for their children, and this imperative can have a profound impact throughout a child's life. "Not only good relationships, but also mature characters are built on appropriate nos."

When our daughter was two, she desired to know about things surrounding us. She would ask many questions, "What's that, mommy?" "Where are we going, mommy?" "How do you spell this, mommy?" and so on. The questions never stopped. Through these years in her life, we could not understand what parents went through when they discussed the "terrible two" years, that is, until our son, Alex, turned two. Alex, who is meticulous and intentional about scientific matters, rarely verbalized his interests. He was our tactile learning child, using his little hands to explore how cause and effect work. Boy, did he give us a run for our money at times! It doesn't surprise me that science is his favorite subject today. We laugh about it now and share those trying times. Alex received many "nos…," with redirection, during his toddler years, and we pray he maintains awareness of godly character and self-discipline, keeping in mind the "no" of yesterday.

It is only natural for children to protest their differences when we try to raise them in a similar manner. When we began homeschooling, we chose a traditional platform and curriculum. Our daughter had readily accepted and adapted to this type of academic learning because she was a visual and auditory learner. When trying the same method on our son, he challenged and protested, seemingly, against everything. His actions revealed his heart. He was a kinesthetic learner who required a hands-on learning experience. We had to be more creative with him and try various methods. Once we incorporated homeschool co-ops, life with homeschooling became less complex. Other teachers could provide an eclectic learning experience but also feed his love for science. We rejoice today because of God's wisdom in meeting the needs of both our children.

As we grow into adulthood, depending on our personality traits, we lose confidence in using a definitive "no." Our upbringing may have taught us that this word has a negative connotation, and perhaps, we think that we will cause more harm than good. Instead, we adopt a pleasant facade rather than telling the simple truth. By these actions, we leave voids and shallow moments in our relationships that require sorting out overtime. Our passivity often fails to accomplish what matters most: a strong, unbreakable relationship.

Using Jesus Christ as a prime example, he and his family sincerely loved one another. However, when he was older, he heightened his "no," not because of their behavior. It was because of their ignorance of his call by the Father. He had to set his mother straight when she disrespected God's timing and authority in his life, at a wedding in Cana (John

2:1-11). His "no" grew louder as he lived closer to fulfill his purpose. His friend Peter used his sword as a threat to the soldier who tried to arrest Jesus. Ironically, Jesus rebuked Peter, putting him in his rightful place and holding him accountable to God's standard of love (John 18:10-11). God's plan is that humanity would experience hope and redemption in Christ Jesus (Rom. 8:6).

A convincing "no" allows mutual respect in any relationship. God specifies His "no" to His children in many aspects of navigating life. Within the proper context, what we tolerate can bring discontentment, inconsistencies, and confusion in our relationships, and "God is not the author of confusion, but of peace" (1 Cor. 14:33).

How often have you been dissatisfied with your relationships because you never spoke honestly about your feelings? Or because you have spoken honestly, you experienced rejection because people weren't ready to receive your transparency? We must decide what we will tolerate because someone refuses to respect who we are. There is a time to be tolerant and a time to be firm in saying, "no." We must be careful not to succumb to people-pleasing and remember that God is with us. He is our guide. Are you intentional about your life? Have you stated a firm "no" when needed, to bring balance in your life?

CONSIDER:

- ✓ In what ways have you learned to say no?
- ✓ How has the truth affected your relationships?

"You're chosen by the One who will never reject you.
You're loved when the crowd cheers and the lights go out,
and they all go home."

JOURNAL #11

How are you making your voice heard in your relationships? Are you setting remarkable boundaries by making your "no" clear? Write down one experience holding true to your value.

Chapter Eight

AN UNDERSTANDING HEART

What is Your Why?

At a young age, our parents taught us how to have compassion for others. My siblings and I were raised in a parsonage on a respected block with decent homes, lush green grass, and giant, beautiful trees. Our beautifully constructed, substantial-sized stone and stained-glass window church, with a spacious parking lot, was located next to our house on a corner lot in Germantown, Pennsylvania. However, there were two astounding mansions two blocks from the parsonage.

Although the houses were beautiful on the outside, from an eight-year-old's viewpoint, the people were eerie and mysterious. They were both young and old and were mentally ill. They walked around with cigarettes in their mouths, unconcerned, apathetic, and slow-moving. However, although sick, their families invested financially in their home life, so that they could live a satisfactory life.

Reflecting on my mother's life, she was a woman of character, gracious, loving, courageous, with heartfelt values, compassion, and inner strength. She had a passion for helping people who needed love, support and encouragement. These people would often walk past our home and occasionally visit our church. Some would ask for a match to light their cigarette, and others would converse with us. I'll never forget one woman who had a lovely voice and would sing to us as if she were ministering to a church congregation. As young people, we did not mock her; instead, we embraced one of her strengths, her voice.

No matter what mental illness these people had, we never saw them as inferior, or a threat. Our parents taught us to pray for them and treat them respectfully. Through our mother's interactions, we learned that God loves humanity. Race, gender, size, socioeconomic background, church affiliation, and other factors did not matter. We were taught that God is impartial; therefore, He extends His love to everyone. He meets people where they are, and He calls us to serve people without judgment.

As believers in Christ, our calling is to be conduits of love and faith. We listen, pray, and provide for others' needs as God makes provision for us. Mostly, our prayer should be that people's lives and circumstances will change. Our mother understood her "why." Today, I understand my "why." What is your why? "If we want to feel an undying passion for our work, if we want to feel we are contributing to something bigger than ourselves, we all need to know our WHY."

CONSIDER:

- ✓ What is your why?
- ✓ Are you living out your God-given purpose?

"For nothing will be impossible with God" (Luke 1:37).

JOURNAL #12

What is your why? Do you understand your gifts to the church? How are you living out your purpose?

Chapter Nine

A DELIBERATE HEART

Who's In Your Circle?

Many people enter our lives, whether through biological, social, or cultural connections. As we mature, we decide who will accompany us or who we will release. At some point, we learn that not all friendships are healthy. God has given us the Holy Spirit to help us sense His direction and wisdom, enabling us to discern between good and evil. What is beneficial for one person may not be helpful for another. He also teaches us the importance of authenticity in our relationships. There are lessons in every relationship, from an acquaintance to a sister-friend. Jesus dealt with various personality traits in his relationships. He discerned the hearts of those around him and questioned them accordingly. "Some people are meant to be lessons rather than life-long companions." However, we must appreciate everyone who enters our lives, after all, we are all God's creation. Some are meant to last forever, a season, or just for a moment.

We see throughout Scripture those who were Jesus' friends, casual and close. All of his disciples were in his life because of the will of the Father. Those who have come into your life are there to impact, inspire, improve, or inquire.

Impact: These people have a high interest in you spiritually, emotionally, and physically. They are willing to go the extra mile to help you get to the next level in life. My advisor is an amazing Spirit-filled woman who has ministered to me in countless ways. She has challenged me to be thoughtful in what I take on to ensure a smooth process academically. She has prayed and offered Scripture to encourage me, given advice and direction when needed, and listened to my woes and regrets. She is wise, direct, and insightful. She has also been in my shoes in various areas throughout her life. She is Godsent and relates to me at many levels of action. "Without counsel plans fail, but with many advisers they succeed" (Prov. 15:22).

Inspire: My young adult children inspire me! They have always looked out for me in more ways than one. There is an understanding that one who has poured themselves out into another receives back fourfold the love shared. I'll never forget the time the homeschool co-op we attended asked me to teach. Previously, I was reluctant to teach with everything I had taken on at the time, but by God's guidance and through my children's inspiration, I said, "Yes!" It was the best thing I could do to enhance their learning, and mine. "And these words that I command you today shall be on your heart. You shall teach them diligently to your children and shall talk of them when you sit in your house, and when you walk by the way, and when you lie down, and when you rise" (Deut. 6:6-7). Children reciprocate what was given to them. If you inspire them, they will eventually inspire you!

Improve: My husband is none other than a man who is forever improving himself. I love this about him because he wishes this for everyone he encounters. No wonder God has placed him in positions to enhance areas in various organizations. His leadership has meant a great deal to our family. Whether it is physically, mentally, emotionally, or spiritually, he desires improvement for himself and us and will provide the means to get us to where we need to be. God has used him as a conduit of strength and purpose in our family, and I'm extremely grateful to the Lord. He is my accountability to maintain focus on what matters most, God's will. He is a constant reminder of leading with purpose. When our kids were entering high school, God knew what I needed most as a homeschooling mom, someone to put in place a plan to help our children reach their next level in school years, and boy, did God come through! Greg put together an excellent plan, and our children thrived in their homeschool, high school years. God's marvelous work is showing itself in their lives today. "Let the wise hear and increase in learning, and the one who understands obtain guidance," (Prov. 1:5).

Inquire: I appreciate the wisdom of my counselor. It is challenging to find someone who understands your background and can sense where you are going. She is blessed with faith, wisdom, and insight. She inquires constructively and thoughtfully, providing instruction through discernment. "The purpose in a man's heart is like deep water, but a man of understanding will draw it out" (Prov. 20:5).

Where do you fit in these categories? Are you impacting others' lives by prioritizing next-level steps for the future? Are you inspiring others to go the extra mile? Are you making improvements in every area of your life and helping others improve theirs as well? Are you concerned about others and inquiring to provide accountability and unlimited possibilities in their lives?

What motivates one to settle for relationships that are not mutually beneficial? Our journey reveals our needs, and over time, it will establish us in these areas or prove the deficiencies we have for readjustment. God makes known His heart to us as we open our hearts to Him. He will provide us with laser eyes to see beyond the surface and eliminate what is unwelcomed. *"In life's journey, we discover who we are, how we are wired, and why we exist."* If we are open to God's will, He will reveal who He is every step of the way. "The steps of a good man are ordered by the Lord, And He delights in his way. (Ps. 27:33).

In my twenties, my most incredible friendships involved personal conversations about God, life, ideas, church, and work. Did we challenge each other? Absolutely!

However, we kept in mind the breath of life. This aspect of my relationships was of most value.

God desires that we live a faithful, Spirit-filled life. To live and please another human being has no value. In this, we fall short of God’s glory and must confess our unfaithfulness to Him. God's love is affirming, convincing, satisfying, and full of promise! Are you deliberate in making wise decisions in your relationships that will lead to a brighter future? Who is in your circle?

CONSIDER:

- ✓ Are you concerned about releasing others who are draining your energy?
- ✓ Are you ready to embrace an improved life?
- ✓ Are you having a difficult time decluttering within your circle of friendships?
- ✓ Keep in mind: Moving forward toward a well-balanced and transformed life is God's will (Rom. 12:2). You owe it to God. You owe it to yourself. You owe it to others. You owe it to your future.

"As iron sharpens iron, so a man sharpens the countenance of his friend" (Prov. 27:17).

JOURNAL #13

Who's in your circle? Are they pushing you further into your purpose, or are they diminishing your purpose?

Chapter Ten

AN AUTHENTIC HEART

What Do You Value?

Oxford Languages Dictionary defines value as the regard that something is held to deserve; the importance, worth, or usefulness of something... a person's principles or standards of behavior; one's judgment of what is important in life.

If you have not assessed your values, anyone can come along and indoctrinate you with what is dear to their heart. As I think about the time when I was teaching a group of fifth-grade students, I asked a question about each student's likes regarding their favorite food, color, etc. One boy in the class would answer, "I don't know." No matter what question of options I gave, he would reply, "I don't know." I had to remind him that God created him in His image, and He is okay with him having likes and dislikes. I also shared how God has likes and dislikes. I mentioned, "Even if you can't come to a decision of what food, color, car, etc., you like, it's better to choose something." We are given options in life, but if we cannot assess our values, someone else will project their values on us. I had to remind him of God's love and God's goodness in him.

Values come from the heart. Our beliefs give us our core values. Values also establish boundaries. They prove what is dear to our hearts. They allow us and others to consider and respect our beliefs, personal preferences, judgments, opinions, etc. As time progressed, this young boy began choosing options that he favored. He drew inferences about himself based on his beliefs, upbringing, likes and dislikes. Over time, he began to recognize his options and valuing his choices became more manageable.

I remember talking to a woman about a relationship she was involved in. She was very dissatisfied, but because of the time she had put into the relationship, she continued to pursue love. How many times have you pursued love based on what you believed was wasted time? She had mentioned that the guy she had come to love did not like or consider her culture's food. She said, "I don't worry; I cook what he likes, so he is happy." She added, "by the way, I do like his culture's food, too." I asked her nicely what she likes most about her culture's food. She replied, "it is where I come from. "It is unique in taste, look, and smell." "It is delicious!" As she had spoken, she gleamed nostalgically, with love and satisfaction.

I asked her if she valued his upbringing and culture better than hers. She stated, "Absolutely not." I asked her if she was willing to trade in her cultural values for his cultural values. She replied, "not at all." I asked her where she found strength and delight in life. What is her lasting memory of her cultural traditions? She intently thought about these questions and lit up as she shared some of her experiences. She needed to be thoughtful of her values. No one else will value anything about you if you don't value your system of beliefs and experiences. Values are created from conception—some change as we mature, but many are held dear to our hearts.

Our socialization, beliefs, cultural traditions, and other experiences impact our lives. Maturity takes place as we explore and appreciate our beliefs and values. No one should discount them or take them away from us. Young or old, relationships should be an even exchange. We must be intentional in what we allow.

CONSIDER:

- ✓ Who or what do you value?
- ✓ Are you planning to date?
- ✓ What is your ideal person?
- ✓ Who would be compatible with you?
- ✓ Are personality traits important in your relationships?
- ✓ Write down your values.
- ✓ Are you looking for a home? Before you start looking, write down what you value in a home.
- ✓ How about a church? What do you value about the church community?
- ✓ Are you aware of your God-given gifts?

"Try not to be a man of success,
but rather try to become a person of value."

JOURNAL #14

What are your personal values? Write a list of what you value, and do not ever settle for less than God's best.

Chapter Eleven

A SURRENDERED HEART

When will you say, "YES!"

"Learn to say 'no' to the good so you can say 'yes' to the best."

There are times in our journey when it is essential that we intentionally voice our "no." On the other hand, our "yes" is just as important. "Yes," implies a willingness to accomplish things that you've contemplated, but perhaps did not have the time or opportunity to fulfill. Perhaps, even fear set in, and therefore, you resisted the challenge. There are seasons when our "yes" is in the flow of life, enjoying the manifestations of what these seasons bring. Also, we experience seasons when our "yes" is only for a moment. Ultimately, our "yes" should benefit others, as we also are benefiting in the process.

As I reflect on my high school years, I remember wanting to play basketball, but I lacked the experience and was a bit too timid to join the team. After graduating high school and deciding to go to college a few years later, I took the plunge and followed an inner dream by joining my college basketball team. I worked hard to know the sport and completed the season, but I determined it was not for me. All in all, my "yes" was completed, and I enjoyed each moment of learning a new skill, engaging with others, and the reward of fulfilling a goal.

During my young adult years, I found myself saying "yes" to every opportunity that came my way. Even if it was only for a season, I was secure in my "yes". Some opportunities were beneficial, and others flopped. I never complained because I knew that the Lord was with me even when things did not work out. I also knew that there was a lesson to be learned from every opportunity. So, I looked for the lesson in the experience, rather than complaining about my weaknesses or the unknown. I always moved on to the next thing, knowing that a greater opportunity was ahead.

I'll never forget a season when I was asked to teach in a homeschool co-op. I was in seminary, homeschooling my kids, and experienced bouts of depression, although still productive. It was one of the most difficult seasons for me, and I made every excuse as to why I couldn't say "yes." I had met many wonderful people who were like-minded and who understood my life at the time. Although I said "no" the first time I was asked, another opportunity was extended to me the following year. In this season, God used my children to say, "Mom, you can do what these moms are doing." Ha!! I put on my momma shoes, prayed, and said an affirmative "yes," and God's blessings followed me.

2 Corinthians 1:20 says, "For all the promises of God in Him are 'Yes', and in Him, Amen, to the glory of God through us." This verse speaks of God's work in His people. He is the "YES" in all we do. In His "yes", there is salvation in Christ Jesus, sanctification, being set apart to walk in His promises, fellowship with like-minded people, experiencing His everlasting love, joy, peace, goodness, forgiveness, hope, heaven, and more! We don't have to second-guess what He provides. As we walk purposefully, we are blessed. He is the "Yes" of all possibilities! The "Amen" in His "yes" signifies closure and affirmation. Therefore, we rest in His promises and live for His glory, honor, and praise.

CONSIDER:

- ✓ Are you struggling to find your "yes" in life?
- ✓ Do you have the peace of God as you walk purposefully in helping others?
- ✓ Are you taking advantage of all the great opportunities presented to you?

When we trust in the Lord, He helps us to stretch our "yes" muscles. When we trust God's process, we regain strength for today and bright hope for tomorrow. When we trust God's plan, we witness His deliverance, His power, and His peace.

JOURNAL #15

What are some reasons you are delaying your "yes"? What are ways you can make your "yes" a reality?

Chapter Twelve

AN ASSURED HEART

Are You Building?

"Little becomes much when we place it in the Master's hands." I remember these words from a song I learned as a young adult called *Ordinary People*. God uses those who desire to be used at any given time. Are you building on what you have already established? Are you increasing your creativity while appreciating what has already been attained?

Catherine Booth, known as the mother of the Salvation Army, was tested and tried many times, but did not quit. She preached during a time when women were disqualified from public ministry. She wrote a pamphlet in 1859 on behalf of a sister in the ministry, Pheobe Palmer, called *Female Ministry: Women's Right to Preach the Gospel.* She became a partner with her husband in preaching the gospel of Jesus Christ and formed a ministry to the poor, which led to what we know today as The Salvation Army, where many lives have been changed and continues to flourish.

Michael Jordan speaks of his many failures before becoming one of the highly regarded basketball players of all time. He says, "Success is built on public failure, painful losses, and moments where your confidence gets shattered. He admits to missing over 9,000 shots, losing nearly 300 games, and failing 26 times when trusted to take the final shot — and says that's exactly why he succeeds." He explains how "pressure, doubt, and adversity forged his mentality, not trophies or highlight reels." However, he is successful today because he continued to build on what had already been foundational.

Author Carol S. Dweck says in her book, *Mindset, The New Psychology of Success*, “Think of times other people outdid you and you just assumed they were smarter or more talented. Now consider the idea that they just used better strategies, taught themselves more, practiced harder, and worked their way through obstacles.” No one is limited by failure or losses; a steady process of building allows one to progress no matter what obstacles he or she faces.

To build is not simply to secure the wood with nails; it is establishing roots that will last a lifetime and benefit future generations. "For every house is built by someone, but He who built all things is God” (Heb. 3:4). Are you allowing the Lord to order your steps? Do you compare yourself to others based on their steps? The Bible tells us that comparisons are unwise.

Are you sharing your expertise or experiences with someone else? Leadership comprises building. Jesus was a master leader. He built wherever he went. The fruit of your labor will be established by the Lord (John 15:16). Are you learning from others? We gain knowledge and wisdom as we observe their success. God plants ideas and gives us strength to achieve great results. Whatever He has impressed on your heart, build! The light at the end of the tunnel is not as crucial as the careful steps taken to get through the tunnel. God controls life, and there is time for improvement while you are still breathing. So, build with respect for God and life. Set small goals, choose an accountability partner, and take baby steps, and you will experience fruit worth sharing, living, and fulfilling!

CONSIDER:

- ✓ Are you building on what you've started?
- ✓ What will it take for you to rebuild?
- ✓ Are you learning from those who have success stories?
- ✓ How are they impacting your life?

"The secret of change is to focus all of your energy not on fighting the old, but on building the new."

JOURNAL #16

Are you building on what you already have? What foundation are you building on? How are you moving forward?

Chapter Thirteen

PURPOSE IN HEART

Why are You Here?

What is your purpose? In other words, why do you exist? What is God's will for your life? Another way to ask this question is how are you serving others? In what areas do you exercise your strengths and passions? Go back 20 - 30 years and reflect on the one thing that made you excited about helping others. What intrigued you about what you were doing? Did you have joy while doing it? Did you feel that you could do it forever? "In life's journey, we discover who we are, how we are wired, and why we exist."

God, the Creator of the Universe, has the key to your life's purpose. It begins with how you were created. God created man in his image, to worship Him. As we seek His wisdom, He guides us in all matters of life. With worship comes service. Who are you serving?

As babies, our parents served us by grooming, pruning, and teaching us how to live. When we enter the world, light exposes us to the beauty of colorful, visual, and spacious surroundings. Our eyes are barely open, but we sense, see, feel, and hear the world differently from the wet and dark comforts of our mother's womb. God is the intelligent designer behind our conception. When we acknowledge that He gave us life, we gain purpose.

God's purpose is designed for us to relate to Him in several aspects taken from Matt. 22:37-38.

1. Know God: Without knowing the Creator, how can one understand who they are and how they should relate to others? The Bible, the number one best seller of all times, teaches that God has called us to serve and worship Him as Creator. In doing so, we must understand His character (Ps. 119:105; Matt 4:4; 2 Tim. 3:16-17) and how we can better relate to His creation. Briefly, in God's will, "He has called us to be saved (1 Tim.2:3, 4), Spirit-fill (v.18), sanctified (1Thess. 4:3), submissive (1 Pet. 2:13-15), suffering (1 Pet. 2:20) and thankful (1 Thess. 5:18). Jesus is our supreme example."

2. Know Self: Our purpose is to understand how God has created, wired, and gifted us. The Holy Spirit gives us knowledge and discernment. He uses many means to help us know ourselves. Personality assessments and gifts assessments have been compiled to help one understand their temperament, behavior patterns, and how we interact with others. These assessments can help one understand his or her strengths. Keep in mind that these are generally true based on much research.

- ✓ https://www.connectassessment.com
- ✓ https://www.16personalities.com/personality-types
- ✓ https://www.lifeway.com/en/articles/women-leadership-spiritual-gifts-growth-service

3. Know Others: God expects us to serve others as Jesus was the ultimate model of service (Mark 10:45; Mark 9:35). His heart of compassion demonstrates God's love for the world. Check out his interactions with others in the gospels. Getting to know others speaks of our relationships in general. Your purpose may be to raise your children and do all you can to teach them God's character and their fit in the world (Deut. 6: 6-9). Administration may be your interest (1 Cor. 12:28). Working with your hands and having a heart to make the industry profitable may be your purpose. Are you passionate about social sciences? God will use you to produce change in others' mental, emotional, and physical state. Do you work in manufacturing or agriculture? Be diligent in working with your hands and treat your customers fairly, and you will be blessed. If it's in science, God will use you to bring good health and wellness to others. Engineering can bring your company good production and sales. If it's ministry, you will be able to equip others for the work God has called them to do. You get the picture! No matter what you do in life, if you have surrendered your life to the Lord, you will be purposeful and blessed while serving others (Col. 3:23).

CONSIDER:

- ✓ Are you living a life worthy of God's call?
- ✓ How are you living out the purpose He has set in your heart?
- ✓ Are you loving others the way you love yourself?
- ✓ Are you seeing others through God's eyes?

If you struggle to identify your purpose, be reminded that it is God-given. It comes naturally as we give our hearts to the Lord and trust His process in our lives.

JOURNAL #17

Are you taking time to understand how God wired you. How is He speaking to you? How is your life reflecting His goodness, so that others are being changed by what they see in you?

Chapter Fourteen

CONFRONTING YOUR HEART

Fear: Where Are You?

Interestingly, God had given Adam and Eve everything their hearts could possibly desire in the Garden of Eden. In that same love, He gave them the fullness of life to draw from Him. He also gave them the freedom to choose death. They were born into perfection, but they could choose imperfection. You may ask, how could they ever have messed that up? Who could mess up perfection when you have never been exposed to imperfection? You guessed right, human beings who are given "free will."

A counselor once told me that children don't have to find evil in this world of sin; evil will find them. The Bible confirms this truth through Adam and Eve's experience. After the Fall, every form of evil pervaded the earth. The Bible is clear that "All have sinned and all fall short of God's glory" (Rom. 3:23). With that said, when children embrace a great foundation in the Lord, they can learn how to dispel evil through God's presence (Deut. 6:6-9). I am not stating that they will live a perfect life or that nothing will harm them. But God will be their sustaining power, and they can overcome any situation life brings. Dr. David Jeremiah said, “The storm is built to make us stronger, wiser, and productive.” Proverbs 24:10 tells us, “If you faint in the day of adversity, your strength is small.” In other words, when we give in to our fears, rather than replace them with faith, spiritual maturity is delayed.

The first evidence of negative emotions appearing on earth was when Adam experienced fear. After he and his wife had been deceived by the evil One and had eaten the forbidden fruit, God, knowing everything, said to Adam, "Where are you?” This question wasn't for God to know Adam's whereabouts. He is all-knowing. It was for Adam to do some introspection to expose his own unfaithful heart. Responsibility is crucial when we are confronted by God.

Adam had lost his identity. He had failed to keep God's rule in his heart and deliberately disobeyed God's will. What made that forbidden tree look more pleasant to the eyes? Interestingly, it was called, the “tree of good and evil.” The Garden of Eden was filled with edible, extraordinary fruit trees. The tree of life was also amid the garden (Gen. 2:9). God asked Adam, "Where Are You?" Adam answered God's question by stating, "Lord, I was afraid. Therefore, I hid." Here's where the rubber meets the road. "I was afraid." Fear entered Adam's heart the moment he sinned against God.

Many people experience fear; therefore, they hide. They hide from the unknown, believing they will be exposed in some way or another of their human flaws. Adam and Eve tried to cover their sin, but God himself exposed their sin of pride. Pride leads to fear, fear of God, self, and others. It can do serious damage to our human psyche if we allow it. The enemy places many excuses in front of us, and the excuses are exaggerated until we are embodied with fear. One huge lie the enemy plants in the heart of hurting believers is that they are unloved. This is far from the truth. The Bible says to put on faith because perfect love cast out fear (1 John 4:18). Fear deprives a person from God's presence.

There are healthy and unhealthy fears. Healthy fear can catapult us in areas that we felt we could never achieve. As an athlete, I may experience fear, but I know if I push through my fear, there is a great reward on the other side. I may encounter fears at work, but I continue to press on because there is a monetary reward waiting that will enhance my living. Whatever coping mechanism I use at work, it somehow releases my fear, and I continue to press through the opposition. As I mentioned earlier, fear can also paralyze us, but only if we allow it. It can be manifested in various ways.

In his book *Deadly Emotions*, Dr. Don Colbert states:

> When you sense your heart filling with fear or your mind crowding with thoughts of irreversible loss, take a minute to ask yourself, 'What right now seems to be fueling this fear?' As best you can, pinpoint the cause of your stress and the source of the fear. And then seek to deal with those issues.

Confronting our fears will allow for clarity, contentment, and further productivity and progression in life.

Deadly emotions can deprive one of a fulfilled life. We must do whatever it takes to surrender our lives to the Lord to live purposefully. If it means getting help, do so. If it means more introspection, take the time to assess what is in your heart and have meaningful conversations, and write down your thoughts. If it means more accountability, take courageous steps closer to a familiar or unfamiliar community. Try new things. There is life in front of you, but you must act responsibly and take care of yourself. Little steps are better than none.

CONSIDER:

- ✓ Are you hiding because of your fears?
- ✓ What is holding you back from confronting your fears?
- ✓ What is holding you back from seeking counsel and sorting out where your fear is coming from?

"The person who measures things by the circumstances of the hour is filled with fear; The person who sees Jehovah enthroned and governing has no panic."

JOURNAL #18

How are you confronting your fears?

Chapter Fifteen

CONTROLLING YOUR HEART

Are You Angry?

Sometimes, we get downright angry! Human! In the flesh! "Anger is a strong emotion of irritation or agitation that occurs when a need or expectation is not met." It is a warning that something is going on within us. Or a feeling or cue that something isn't right. So how do we handle what is going on within us? We must balance our feelings so that they do not conquer us. We have a choice. We can let our anger break us or move with action and deal with what we are feeling.

Our conditioned mindset can distort our sensory data. It can also distort the truth of what's really going on inside. Man's truth is subjective. Therefore, we must weigh our feelings against what we know is true. We weigh our actions according to God's Word. We may simply ask, how did Jesus feel when the devil was tempting him beyond measures during his wilderness experience? We may ask, at what level was Jesus' temptation when he overthrew the tables in the temple, yet without sin? We may need to ask ourselves, how concerned is God and where is He amid our troubles? We may also consider our upbringing and ask; how did I deflect my anger in past situations? What brought on this feeling? How do I embrace this feeling and work to get back on the right track?

We may need to ask ourselves questions to sort out what we feel. What we ask ourselves can change the trajectory of our response. How do you process your anger? What steps have you taken to resolve your anger? Have you learned to deflect, project, or deny what you feel? Have you learned to flat out confront your anger? According to Scripture, anger is not sinful. However, what we do with our anger can harm us and others physically, emotionally, or spiritually.

Cain was the eldest in his family, and he had a younger brother named Abel. However, Cain became so angry and envious of Abel because God said Cain's offering was not acceptable and Abel's offering was. Hebrews 11:4 states, "By faith Abel offered God a better sacrifice than Cain did. By faith he was commended as a righteous man, when God spoke well of his offerings."

Cain was angry. What was in Cain's heart that allowed him to feel dejected? Did he fail himself? Was he so prideful and in denial of his resistance to obeying God's will? Sibling rivalry comes with a twist in families. Competition can play a huge part in these relationships. It is human instinct to deal with others competitively. The eldest may try to convince herself and everyone else that she is worthy of respect due to her seniority. Over time, the younger of the two may resist this control to prove herself worthy of respect as a human being. Families deal with many issues, but no matter what the issue, both present a problem by projecting their anger on each other.

There are many factors when it comes to conflict in our relationships. However, God is the ultimate deciding factor amid inner and outer conflicts. God graciously asked Cain about his anger. He called Cain's appearance out. "Why has your countenance fallen" (Gen. 4:6)? Amongst other reasons, our appearance can reveal our dissatisfaction. Whether we show what we are feeling or not, God sees our heart. Nothing is hidden from Him. He will call out our lack of obedience to His will. He said to Cain, "If you do well, will you not be accepted?" There was an identity crisis at hand, for Cain. God asked a legitimate question. I believe that God was conveying that Cain would do well, if he would just obey Him in heart, mind, and spirit. God knew that Cain was about to destroy his future. He knew that Cain would allow his anger to go beyond his attitude. He knew that Cain would eventually kill his brother, Abel. God was trying to protect Cain from his own flesh. However, Cain rejected God's voice.

We all need accountability. We need others to call us to the carpet sometimes. Cain's anger and resistance to God's voice led him into a downward spiral. This type of anger is sinful and will destroy us.

- ✓ Are you wearing sinful anger?
- ✓ What kind of questions are you asking yourself regarding your anger?
- ✓ Is there a fire burning in your heart?
- ✓ Are you allowing God to speak to your heart through His Word, people, or circumstances?
- ✓ Can you discern the controlling factors that are delaying your progress?
- ✓ Are you walking in obedience to God's will in heart, mind, and spirit?

Dr. Gary Collins, a Christian Counselor, gives several helpful conclusions about human anger.

- **Human Anger Can Be Controlled.** It is unlikely that God would have instructed us to control anger if human anger control was impossible.
- **Anger Must Be Acknowledged.** Before we can 'put away' our bitterness, wrath, anger, and malice, we must admit, at least to ourselves, that these feelings exist.
- **Outbursts Must Be Restrained.** The man or woman of God thinks before acting. There must be a quiet weighing

of issues instead of a gushing forth of sinful verbal explosions.

“Sometimes, it is helpful to share one’s burden of anger with a friend; it is always good to pour out one’s feelings to God. This verbal activity often leads to new perspectives that reduce or dissipate anger before it is expressed inappropriately and allowed to harm others or damage relationships.”

CONSIDER:

- ✓ Do you run to God when you are burning with anger?
- ✓ How have you learned to redirect your anger?
- ✓ Do you have someone to hold you accountable in resolving your anger?

"Human anger is designed by God to motivate us to take constructive action in the face of wrongdoing or when facing injustice."

JOURNAL #19

Is anger holding you back from moving further into God's purpose in your life? What are key ways you intend to resolve your anger?

Chapter Sixteen

TRAINING YOUR HEART

Why Worry?

In her book on worry, June Hunt says, "Worry is mental distress primarily over a negative possibility in the future. It is a state of mind, a way of thinking, a mental habit." Dr. Don Colbert writes,

> About nineteen million Americans suffer from anxiety disorders, but far more suffer from mild anxiety that has not yet developed to the disorder state. Experiencing severe or continual anxiety isn't necessarily pathological-meaning that a person has an emotional or mental disturbance. In many of these people, worry has simply become a mental habit. They automatically tend to see events in their lives in terms of worst-case scenarios.

The Psalmist wrote, "My thoughts trouble me, and I am distraught" (Ps. 55:2). What makes us worry when we are witnesses of God's provision in Creation? Did He not create the birds of the air to find food and feed themselves? Did he not clothe the beautiful lilies of the field? These provisions are from God. Only God can sustain our lives. We are subject to Him in all things. The simple answer to our worry is that we are imperfect people trying to regain a perfect connection to the perfect God, who created us in His image.

Our thought patterns are difficult to break because we get stuck, and it is difficult for us to be convinced otherwise. We worry about our kid's struggles, young or old, a broken marriage, terminal illness, finances, church dysfunction, grief, family quarrels, a traumatic event, etc. The mind tends to rehearse events beyond our control, convincing us that we will eventually gain control of our circumstances. By practice, if not careful, worry can subtly draw us into dysfunction, leading to death. "Peace, I leave with you, My peace I give to you; not as the world gives do I give to you. Let not your heart be troubled, neither let it be afraid" (John 14:27).

Adam and Eve disgraced God by disregarding His voice, and worry filled their lives. Some people worry because it is easier to worry than to seek help or break the mental habit by walking through the process with God's truth. Some people worry because they have conditioned themselves to rehearse bothersome events.

If general worry is habit-forming, we can recondition ourselves to trust God for His providence over life. He gives choice in all matters of life. He allows us to continue to lean on our own understanding, until we are broken. Or we can simply trust his process as the birds of the air and the lilies of the field. Nothing is easy. Any habit requires work. Jesus says, "Come to me, all who labor and are heavy laden, and I will give you rest. Take my yoke upon you, and learn from me, for I am gentle and lowly in heart, and you will find rest for your souls. For my yoke is easy, and my burden is light" (Matt. 11:28–30).

The Bible also specifies seasons of change and a time for healing to take place in the hearts of broken people. Understanding our imperfection, God allows humanity time to walk through the process of naturally occurring events. In our journey, we learn He can be trusted even when life seems bleak.

Below are several tips to turn your worry into peace:

1. **Be Proactive!** Confront your worry, and don't let it fester.

✓ **Pray** without ceasing!
✓ **Embrace** vulnerability in a safe space.
✓ **Journal** as you can.
✓ **Seek support** through counseling, coaching, a small group, etc.

2. **Capture** Your Thoughts!

✓ Meditate on what is true, lovely, good report, excellence, and what is praiseworthy (Phil. 4:6-8).
✓ Memorizing Scripture brings life to all who receive it.
✓ Get mediation if necessary!
✓ Read:
Scriptures on Worry/Anxiety
Articles on how others have overcome worry
Books on worry such as *Worry*, by June Hunt or
Deadly Emotions, by Dr. Don Colbert

Never forget to be of good cheer! God is with you.

CONSIDER:

- ✓ How does it make you feel to know that worry is a mental habit?
- ✓ Have you considered how much time you have allowed yourself to worry over what may or may not change?
- ✓ Have you tried various steps to turn your worry into peace? The Bible says that we can casts all of our cares on the Lord because He cares for us (1 Pet. 5:7).
- ✓ Will you take steps to cast your cares on the Lord?
- ✓ Have you thought about treating your worry habit as a general habit that can be broken within twenty-one days depending on the circumstance? Some worry habits will take longer. Give it a try!
- ✓ Check out the book, *Atomic Habits,* by James Clear. You will be glad you did.

"Let us therefore come boldly to the throne of grace, that we may obtain mercy and find grace to help in time of need" (Heb. 4:16).

JOURNAL #20

Who/what are you allowing to control your life?
How will you take time to conquer your worry habit?

PART III
LIFE REASSURING ANCHOR

"This *hope* we have as an anchor of the soul, both sure and steadfast…" (Heb. 6:19).

Chapter Seventeen

A WHOLE HEART

"I will praise You, O Lord, with my whole heart; I will tell of all Your marvelous works" (Ps. 9:1).

In his "I will" statement, the Psalmist has concluded, from the depth of his heart, that he owes God every ounce of worship due to Him. He determines that he should declare and give his voice and life to no one else but God for all the marvelous works He has done.

The heart is a delicate part of our being. It tells the stories of our journey, including our joys and sorrows. It says something different about each person. God is not surprised by the stories in our journey, whether good or bad. He understands our coming and going. He is aware of everything that has happened in our lives. The Psalmist declares that our praises should be centered on the Creator and His magnificent works in our lives. After all, He owns everything! He produces the rhythms of the physical heart. He determines the timing within each beat, the pulse, the flow of blood, and oxygen. Every organ has a specific purpose. The same is true with plants and animals. It is with the mouth that we acknowledge God's existence and His Sovereignty over the universe.

The heart also reveals whether we are conforming to God's character (Ps. 119:11). In every move we make, people observe our lives to see whether our characteristics are aligned with Christ. Yes, they mock, sabotage, criticize, project, lie, compete, and compare. They did it to our Lord;

why wouldn't they do it to us? Although we are being sanctified daily, we must continue to walk as wise stewards of our lives and give the Lord glory for all that He has done.

When the Pharisees were disturbed by the multitude's worship of Jesus, and wanted him to rebuke his disciples, as they worshipped him, Jesus replied to them saying, "I tell you that if these should keep silent, the stones would immediately cry out" (Luke 19:40). Even when we are not cooperative of praising the Lord, nature will rise up and give Him the honor that is due.

In my conversations, I find myself spontaneously including the Lord's name, because He is my all. Whatever has been planted in your heart will automatically be revealed. There is no performance in authentic acknowledgement of God's presence. Jeremiah said it this way, "Then I said, I will not make mention of Him, nor speak anymore in His name. But His Word was in my heart like a burning fire shut up in my bones; I was weary of holding it back, And I could not" (Jer. 20:9). The Psalmist in Psalm 9 could not hold back his praises to God. Jeremiah could not contain Him, and if He is in your spiritual DNA, His marvelous works will be proclaimed throughout your life.

CONSIDER:

- ✓ How deep is your love for God?
- ✓ Can you say, as the Psalmist said, an affirmative, "I will" praise the Lord with my whole heart?
- ✓ Are you serving the Lord with your whole heart?
- ✓ Are you like the Psalmist who could not contain God's message and marvelous works?

Lord, help us to consider the emotional heart that you have created in us to praise Your holy name. Destroy every argument that arises in us against your Word. Help us to speak the truth, so that it will be a magnet for your marvelous works. In Jesus' matchless name we pray, Amen.

JOURNAL #21

In what ways are you taking the initiative to give God your whole heart?

Chapter Eighteen

A HEART ALIGNED WITH GOD'S PROVIDENCE

"I will lift up my eyes to the hills-from whence comes my help. My help comes from the Lord, who made the heaven and earth" (Ps. 121).

I'll never forget the days when I was ages 7 through 9. My father was asked to speak in the Pocono Mountains every summer. My family looked forward to this opportunity because it gave us a chance to get away from the city and experience a change of environment. The mountains were beautiful, and the atmosphere was serene. It was a place of reward for us, and we valued it very much.

Another time in the mountains that I'll never forget is when my husband and I were on a Christian retreat. We faced the challenge of climbing a mountain with several other Christian sisters and brothers. This was a difficult task for all of us, but we encouraged one another throughout the climb. Some people became exhausted and dehydrated, and they decided to quit. Others became discouraged because they felt that it was too much to bear. Others continued to climb, not looking left or right, but focusing on the victory ahead. When we reached the mountain's summit, we celebrated and reflected on God's promises. "In everything give thanks, for this is God's will in Christ Jesus concerning you" (1 Thess. 5:18).

Psalm 121 was written to encourage the psalmist during a pilgrimage to the "hills of Jerusalem, in particularly, the temple." It is a song or hymn of ascents: To ascend means to climb to an altitude beyond one's reach. Or soar above whatever is trying to prevent one from succeeding. "'Ascents' translates the Hebrew word *ma'aloth,* which means 'goings up.' These songs may have been 'Pilgrim Psalms' sung by those who were 'going up' to Jerusalem and 'ascending' to the Temple (1 Sam. 1:3; Is. 30:29)." This Psalm reminds the reader to continue striving or persevering through life's most difficult trials. I'm not sure what your dark place or valley may be, or the opposition you have faced, but it encourages one to ascend above anything that hinders one from maintaining focus on God's providential care throughout life.

During his journey, the psalmist is experiencing some anxiety. He is traveling through desert land. He is not only physically exhausted but also threatened by the exposure of elements and the heat. "They could be scorched if they did not find shade." This area is known as a hideout for thieves and for those looking to take advantage of travelers. Despite his fears, the traveler makes a conscious decision to look up and soar past his reality. He is determined, based on what he knows, to trust in the living God and persevere through his emotions. Although God is with us and will forever be with us, we experience heartfelt issues as anxiety, but we must encourage ourselves through song and the Word to be reminded of God's presence.

Amid any obstacle, God promises protection and deliverance for His people. Anxiety will come, but Scripture reminds us to "cast all of our cares on the Lord because He cares for us" (1 Peter 5:7). We should also experience anticipation, believing that God will rescue us. So, continue to look to the hills from which your help comes, knowing that God is dependable. He will help you through any storm or trial. He is our strength. He is our protector. He is forever present.

CONSIDER:

- ✓ Who do you run to when you are experiencing anxious thoughts?
- ✓ Have you been in predicaments where you've felt that you couldn't make it alone?

Lord, when we are feeling anxious, alone, or desperate, help us to remember that You are with us and that we can call on Your name for help in any situation. I pray that we will encourage ourselves with Your word and trust Your presence in our lives. In Jesus' precious name, Amen.

JOURNAL #22

In what ways has the Lord proven to be your Protector and Deliverer?

Chapter Nineteen

A FRIEND IN HEART

"Therefore that disciple whom Jesus loved said to Peter, 'It is the Lord!' Now when Simon Peter heard that it was the Lord, he put on his outer garment (for he had removed it) and plunged into the sea" (John 21:7).

Who would you choose if you had to leave your beloved mother in the hands of a trusted friend? Would it be one who was most loyal to you? Would it be a relative or a non-relative? Or possibly both. Jesus trusted his cousin and best friend, John, to take care of his mother, even more than his stepbrothers, James, Simon, Joseph, and Jude (John 19:20-29).

What made John's life so special that Jesus' trust level for him was profound? The text does not convey why Jesus trusted this disciple more than his brothers. However, we can infer from the Scripture that John's love and dedication to Jesus were evident. Jesus told John, while on the cross, to take care of his mother for the remaining time of her life (John 19:26-27). Jesus held John in the highest esteem among his disciples. He called him "brother." "The words, 'Woman, behold thy son … behold thy mother' are more than a mere commendation or suggestion from a dying friend. They convey a command from Him who was, to Mary, as well as to John, Master and Lord." Jesus had separated himself from the human being he had called mother for 33 years. He was sent on earth to complete the will of his heavenly Father. So much can be said about the first sentence in John 21:7; however, I will digress as I must move further into this powerful verse.

It was after Jesus' resurrection when Jesus appeared to Mary Magdalene, Joanna, Mary the mother of James, and other women (Lk. 24:10), but he told Mary not to cling to him because he had not yet ascended to heaven. He had given them instructions to go and tell the eleven disciples that he would go to the Father, who is God (Jn. 20:17). He is identifying with his true disciples, including Mary and the other women! So, Mary Magdalene and other women were the first indirect disciples to report Jesus' appearance after his resurrection (Jn. 10:3).

Jesus made appearances to his "brethren" as he called them (Jn 20:17), prior to this encounter at the Sea of Tiberias (20:19). Although Jesus showed himself to the disciples, they did not recognize him ashore (21:4). After the command to throw the net on the right side of the boat, and the numerous amounts of fish observed, John immediately recognized and identified him. In comparison to both instances, can you identify Jesus in your life? Do you hear his voice? John loved Jesus because he had invested time in him. The more you invest in knowing the Savior, the more you discern his presence. The disciples needed Jesus to meet a need beyond their scope. They couldn't catch any fish. Have you ever been so excited to see Jesus show up amid a personal situation? Contentment comes from knowing our personal Savior, who is Lord over all creation.

Interestingly, Peter was on the shore, and he did not recognize Jesus. John had to tell the other disciples that it was Jesus on the shore. Community is necessary for every believer. Without it, we are subject to disregarding the obvious. “There is safety in the fellowship of believers” (Prov 11:14-paraphased). Are you the one people depend on to discern the truth? Are you the one who will confidently exclaim, "Jesus is with us!" because you recognize his supernatural power?

Peter covered himself when he realized it was the Lord. Why would he cover himself? What was there to cover when he was already exposed among his friends? "He then plunged into the sea" (John 21:7). Was Peter just above himself? Was he now inspired because he knew something big would take place? Did he now turn into the big kid he was in heart? What will heaven be like for you? Perhaps he was comforted by the knowledge that Jesus would make all things right. When Jesus shows up, nothing is impossible!

CONSIDER:

- ✓ What about you? How is Jesus showing up in your life?
- ✓ Do you even recognize Him?
- ✓ Do you recognize the power of God?
- ✓ There are times in my life that I am doubting Thomas. I need the facts! How about you?
- ✓ Keep in mind that nothing is impossible when you remove pride from your life in exchange for taking pride in knowing the Lord.

Help us, Lord, to remember that the facts aren't always important because you are aware of all our needs. Help us to trust your voice, as Mary did. Give us awareness of your supernatural power as John acquired. Help us to maintain your peace. We need you, Father. In Jesus' precious name, Amen.

JOURNAL #23

How is Jesus showing up in your life?

Chapter Twenty

A WEARY HEART

Jesus Teaches with Understanding

"Come to Me, all you who labor and are heavy laden, and I will give you rest. Take my yoke upon you and learn from Me, for I am gentle and lowly in heart, and you will find rest for your souls. For my yoke is easy, and my burden is light" (Matt. 11:28-30).

Jesus' life resembled his calling. He was the Son of Man; yet he was the Son of God (11:27). He healed the sick. He raised the dead. He solved problems. He rebuked the legalists. He challenged societal beliefs. He perceived the thoughts of every man. In the same breath, he gave understanding (11:28). Jesus spoke of his Father and his call whenever he was given the chance. He opposed the proud but showed grace to those who listened, sought after, and followed him. He spoke the words "Come" with the perception that life is complicated for humanity, and because of this, a person could easily conclude that faith was not for him or her.

Jesus said, "Come" to those who had been crushed by life and needed rescuing. He said, "Come" to those who had been discouraged and confused by societal injustices. "Come" to those who were debilitated and suffering physically, emotionally, and mentally. Bottom line is, Jesus understood that without faith in his oneness with the Father, his works on earth, his suffering, and his resurrection, it would be impossible to satisfy God. He understands your need, and he bore your pain.

A "yoke" symbolizes bondage. In contrast, "rest" represents freedom and peace. Keep in mind, Jesus does not cheer you on by saying, "You can do it!" He says, "Trust me first. You are victorious if you trust me because I am the one who resurrects and gives life to all who will receive it." So, "Come" unto me, and I will provide you with the so-needed "rest" your heart desires. He understood that life would present crushing moments and brokenness, which could lead to a complete denial of any rights we think we deserve. He gives life on earth and eternal life. In taking his yoke upon you, you will understand his suffering during your suffering. In coming to him, you could stand the process if you allow him to meet you where you are. He says to the unbeliever, "Trust me, and you will forever find life." He says to the believer, "I am here at your beck and call, so call on me!"

If you have not chosen to trust Jesus today as the Son of Man, as well as the Son of God, he is waiting for you. If you have trusted him as fully Man and fully God, he cares for you and challenges you to stay on track. The cross is where we must continue to lay down our lives, but because of the resurrection, we must move forward knowing that He is alive and intercedes on our behalf. His yoke is easy. It does not take much. His burden is light because the perfect One has paid it all!

Isn't it good to trust in the only One who can offer rest for your weary heart? Isn't it good to know that you are safe in Jesus' everlasting arms? Salvation provides light and life! Move forward in Christ, knowing that his grace is enough for you yesterday, today, tomorrow, and forever!

CONSIDER:

- ✓ Jesus is sensitive to your heart.
- ✓ He knows the depths of what you feel.
- ✓ He waits for you to call on him.
- ✓ He will respond.

Lord, remove the yoke of bondage that is in the way of worshipping You. Continue to break us so that we will be stretched and strengthened, as when we first came to trust in Jesus. For your glory, honor, and praise. In Jesus' name, Amen.

JOURNAL #24

Is there a special need you have in this phase of life? Write it out. Ask the Lord to provide this need. He will respond.

Chapter Twenty-One

A PEACEFUL HEART

Be anxious for nothing, but in everything by prayer and supplication with thanksgiving let your requests be made known to God And the peace of God, which surpasses all comprehension, will guard your hearts, and your minds in Christ Jesus…Phil. 4:6-7

I am reminded of a time when I had just completed my spring semester in seminary. Prior to this, I was overwhelmed by life's pressures. I had to keep track of my kids homeschool schedule, shop and prepare meals for my family, maintain my home, and ensure that my kids and I completed our semester well. I was burdened by the thought that I would not be able to complete the demands of book reviews, research papers, and final exams. Although I had a month left before the spring semester ended, it seemed as if I would never get there.

Each time I thought of the freedom that would soon come, I was able to breathe and focus on the present, but when I thought of all the tasks before me, I felt anxious as if I was slowly suffocating. It was as if I had a Mary-Martha complex wrapped into one. When Jesus was on his way for a visit to Mary and Martha's home, Mary patiently waited for him to come, while Martha was busily trying to prepare for his coming. I imagine, in a modern sense, she polished the furniture, made the beds, vacuumed the floor, cleaned the bathrooms, cleaned the kitchen, possibly placed items in the attic so that her procrastination wouldn't be exposed, and set it off by diffusing a combination of citrus oils. When Jesus arrived, Mary sat at his feet adoring him. She was amazed by his glowing face, his humility, and his fervent spirit of compassion. She waited immensely for every teachable moment. Martha envied Mary's focus. She self-righteously judged her sister, thinking she, Martha, was on the right path when she had lost herself in the work (Luke 10:38-42).

During my distressed period, I chose to fixate on the end results while allowing the Lord to guide me one step at a time. I had to yield and be prayerful about the "how," while at the same time, be thankful for the platform that God had placed in my life. He has given me a hard-working husband who has allowed me to homeschool my kids. He has allowed me to learn more of His Word by attending seminary. He has allowed me to assist my daughter with her biology labs by dissecting fish, crawfish, frogs, earthworms, and more. He has allowed me to study alongside my son and provide insight during his History, Bible, English, Algebra, Science, and more classes. He has allowed me to have daily conversations with both children about His Word and His work in their lives...He has given me a home we can use and share in unity. He has…the list goes on!

As I reflected on His goodness in my life during this trying season, His peace overflowed my soul! What a great feeling to know that God is with us even in the most pressing times in life. Since then, I have had anxious thoughts, yet when I am still, His settling voice reminds me that He will never leave me, nor forsake me (Heb. 13:5). Yes, it is because of Jesus that I can continually feel the love of God. He guarded my heart and my mind as I reflected on His goodness, and yes, I accomplished all that was before me.

CONSIDER:

God is ever-present.
God is not distant from those he loves.
God is a responsible and orderly God.
God is our peace.

- ✓ We must be prayerful regarding the "how."
- ✓ We must be thankful for all that He has given to us.
- ✓ We must be thoughtful, not allowing life to consume us.

Lord, calm our anxious hearts, so that we will be one with You. Help us to take one day at a time, so that we will experience Your peace. Thank you for the Holy Spirit's leading in our lives. In Jesus' precious name, amen.

JOURNAL #25

Do you have peace in your heart?
Name several experiences that has rob you of God's peace? What have you done to counteract the situation?

Chapter Twenty-Two

A HEART OF PRAISE

"The Lord your God in your midst, The Mighty One, will save; He will rejoice over you with gladness, He will quiet you with His love, He will rejoice over you with singing" (Zephaniah 3:17).

As we have seen throughout Scripture, God is with His people and will forever be in their midst. We have seen Him in Abraham's life, as He had shown Himself faithful in keeping His promise of sending a ram into the bush in place of Isaac's death. As an act of obedience to God, Abraham trusted God's promise and laid Isaac's life down on the altar of sacrifice to give offerings unto the Lord (Gen. 22:8-12). God is a promise-keeper (Heb. 6:18-)! Are you trusting in His promises?

We see in Scripture how God provided food for the Israelites as they traveled forty days and forty nights through the wilderness. He sent manna and quail from heaven so His people would not starve (Ex. 16). He will surely provide you with every need. He provided protection and guidance by sending a cloud by day and a pillar of fire by night (Ex. 13:21-22). He is intentional. He guides us into His will. Has He provided all of your needs according to His riches in glory, through Christ Jesus (Phil. 4:19)?

He destroyed Pharaoh and the Egyptian army and split the Red Sea for His people. He will save His people at all costs. Never fear what people can do to you (Ps. 118:6). God can change what you cannot control (Matt. 10:28). He will rescue you from all harm. Yes, His boast in His people goes unmatched. Are you trusting Him to protect you from all harm?

When we are anxious, He surrounds us with His love (Is. 41:10). We can feel His presence because He exists on our behalf. We can trust His words; they are reassuring. To know God is to have everything needed for life and godliness (2 Pet. 1:3). Never fail to praise our God and spread His forever love to all who desire to know Him. He is our mighty God. He will save His people; He loves and rejoices over us.

CONSIDER:

- ✓ God's presence is with His people. He is mighty to save!
- ✓ His Word protects and strengthens us!
- ✓ Never fail to exalt His name; He honors all who praise Him.

Lord, help us to rely on your promises. Help us to be encouraged and strengthened by your unchanging Word. When we are anxious, help us to give our burdens to you, knowing that you can carry the weight that seems too difficult to bear. In Jesus' precious name, Amen.

JOURNAL #26

Are you aware of God's presence in your life?
What does your heart say about God, the Almighty One?
In what ways have you experienced His enduring love?

Chapter Twenty-Three

A MEEK HEART

"Blessed are the meek, for they shall inherit the earth" (Matt. 5:5).

My mother was a meek woman of integrity. She came from humble beginnings. She was born with anemia, a heart murmur, and as time progressed, it was evident that she had severe scoliosis. She was very sick as a child and a teen and had numerous surgeries. Throughout her life, she learned how to trust God. She was not one who talked much, was not prone to gossip or self-righteous chatter, but she diligently prayed, encouraged, and inspired others. She could admit her imperfection while having an earnest fear of God. She lived a committed life before her children and amid all who had known her.

To be blessed is to be filled with spiritual joy. It is indicative of those who share in the salvation of the Lord. Oxford Languages Dictionary notes meek, as "quiet, gentle, and easily imposed on; a submissive spirit." It illustrates a gentle nature, which is a spiritual fruit (Gal. 5:23). It is characteristic of one who lives a humble and submissive life and is not proud or arrogant.

Meekness depicts one who surrenders his or her will to serve another. It is empowered by self-control, another spiritual fruit (Gal. 5:23). My mother prayed, understanding that only the Master could be effective where she could not. Scripture describes Moses as a "very meek" man (Numbers

12:3). God chose him to confront Pharaoh and lead His people from the hands of the Egyptians (Exodus 2).

Matthew 5:5 says that the meek will "inherit the earth." If one is to "inherit the earth," he or she will be filled with joy and contentment, despite his or her circumstances. When one is meek, he or she is concerned about the welfare of others. He or she does whatever is necessary to provide, protect, and encourage those who are in need. When one is meek, he or she looks forward to the future kingdom, realizing that earth is not his or her home (Phil. 3:20). He or she is guided by the Holy Spirit and points the finger to Jesus and gently walks another by the hand. Yes, my mother was meek. She inherited the earth, and I feel blessed to have been under her care for twenty-eight extraordinary years.

CONSIDER:

✓ Who comes to mind when you think of one that is meek in heart?

Lord, help us to sense the blessings of being meek. Help us to meditate on your Word so that we will humble ourselves before you. Thank you, Lord, for those mothers and fathers who have exhibited the characteristics of meekness. Thank you, Lord, for Jesus Christ! Amen.

JOURNAL #27

Are you striving to be meek in heart?
How is the Lord dealing with you in this area?

Chapter Twenty-Four

A CONSCIENTIOUS HEART

"But whoever causes one of these little ones who believe in Me to stumble, it would be better for him if a millstone were hung around his neck, and he were thrown into the sea" (Mark 9:42).

In Mark 9:36, Jesus said to accept the innocent because when you receive them, you receive him, and when you receive him, you receive the Father. The disciples were on the receiving side. Therefore, to receive one was to defend those who could not protect themselves. Being on the receiving end allows others to walk with discernment and good judgment. Legalistic battles within the faith-based community can infiltrate the innocent and take the emphasis off the character of Christ (Phil 2:5). It causes disruption and confusion (1 Cor 14:33). It tears down the body rather than builds one's security in faith, and it disunifies and distracts the gospel from flourishing.

God takes offense when one causes the innocent to stumble in disbelief. Children are immature, weak, and ignorant of life. In this context, they are considered new believers. Jesus is stating that he despises when children are sacrificed for the pride and unrestraint of others. "In Jesus' analogy, this refers most directly to children (Mark 9:36–37), but the implication is that God will deal with those who mislead other people (compare 10:24)."

Cooper states:

> Our actions and our words carry significant weight. How many of us have caused someone weaker in faith to doubt or to trust in works rather than in Christ? Jesus calls this a heavy yoke. Jesus turned the tables and insisted that it would be better for the offender to be drowned in the sea by a large stone used to grind grain than to cause even one person to doubt or sin.

"A millstone is a stone so large it took a donkey to turn it." Jesus uses strong language here to enforce his words, and remind those who hear to listen carefully. Let's ponder the love of God in this context (Heb. 12:6). God's love is balanced.

"Drowning in the ocean" illustrates a righteous anger. He will judge the perpetrator. God expects His people to depend on Him by praying His will, not opposing His providence in the lives of those among us. God has called His people to be witnesses and ambassadors of truth. Ensuring one's spiritual growth and unity amongst the saints is a mark of Christian maturity.

Keep in mind:
When someone comes into the church community, we must:
✓ Welcome them with open hearts and be careful how we lead them.
✓ Be wise in what we feed them.
✓ Be understanding and sensitive to their pain.

CONSIDER:

- ✓ Are you exercising your faith so that other people's lives are changed?
- ✓ Are you a conscientious learner?

Lord, help us to be like-minded in the body of Christ. Help us to have the mind of Christ in attitude and in deed. Help us to be sensitive to others' needs. Help us to stand for righteousness to protect those around us. Help us not to lean on our own understanding and be wise in our own eyes. Help us to fear you and walk in your wisdom. In Jesus' name, Amen.

JOURNAL #28

Are you aware of the young in heart surrounding you? Are you reflecting God's ways above your ways? How can you responsibly direct one to Christ?

Chapter Twenty-Five

A GENTLE HEART

For depth of narrative, read: John 9:1-12
"And His disciples asked Him, saying, 'Rabbi, who sinned, this man or his parents, that he was born blind'" (John 9:2)?

Although the disciples were with the living God, they failed to know and trust him. They called him "Rabbi." In the Jewish culture, a "Rabbi" is a teacher of the law. Jesus had proven himself to be the trustworthy teacher of everything in life. However, people had always placed limitations on him. He was 100% more than a teacher of the law. They heard his claims as God's Son (John 13:1-19), witnessed his power from above (Matt. 28:18), and adored his teachings against the seekers of the law (Matt 7:12, John 7:16), but their minds could not perceive his majesty.

The disciples were mere men whom Jesus had called to follow and learn from him. They came from various backgrounds and walks of life. Some were poor fishermen; others were thriving tax collectors. However, they were flawed human beings, and Jesus specifically noticed them. Jesus also saw the blind man whom the disciples had inquired about. They asked, "Rabbi, who sinned, this man or his parents, that he was born blind" (v. 2)? They had ignorantly and prematurely accused this man or his parents of sin.

Lesson: We must be careful not to jump to conclusions. When we walk in ignorance and pride, we cheat others and ourselves of blessings. We also distort God's character when we judge someone else's character. Rather than asking Jesus the right question, why was this man born blind from birth? They assumed the blindness was due to some sinful act of the man or his parents. In other words, God is not just; therefore, someone must pay the penalty for this man's blindness. Either the man sinned, or it had to be his parents. Jesus answered, "Neither this man nor his parents sinned, but that the works of God should be revealed in him" (v.3). Never fail to ask the right question, and if you don't know what to ask, keep quiet and leave the answer in the Lord's hands.

Lesson: Sickness does not mean that God is placing judgment on someone's life. God is gracious and forever merciful to those who trust Him. We must know the width, length, height, and depth of God's love (Eph. 3:18). Bottom line, with sin came sickness! The following year, after the COVID outbreak, many were ashamed to mention that they had COVID-19 because people feared the accusations they would face. Be wise. Be humble.

Lesson: Even in sickness, our lives will reflect God's glory. He uses the pain from original sin to bring others into the knowledge of His truth. Remember that everything that happens in our lives is to bring glory to Jesus Christ. Brokenness brings glory to Christ. Rejection brings us closer to Christ. Healing points the finger to Christ. If we are genuinely Christ-centered, we live to bring glory to Christ. Also, it is okay to ask people to pray but ask those who will pray and not use your sickness or pain to their advantage.

CONSIDER:

- ✓ We must always ensure that our theology is correct, so we do not defile God's Word with worldly thinking and minimize God's thoughts with mere speculatory claims.
- ✓ We must continue to study to show ourselves approved unto God so that we do not walk according to our own history and project our feelings or personal beliefs upon others.
- ✓ We must pray, walk in humility, and inquire with the right questions. Jesus' thinking is above our immature speculations.

Lord, help us not to think so highly of ourselves that we are accusatory in our claims against another. Help us to walk with humility and balanced teaching so that we will please you with our mind, will, and emotion. Thank you, Lord, for the authority of your Word. It is reassuring. It is refreshing. It is life-giving! In Jesus' name, Amen.

JOURNAL #29

Have you ever dealt with an illness of some kind and have experienced the scrutiny of others because of it? How did it make you feel? How did you discern God's voice amid your suffering?

Chapter Twenty-Six

A GOOD HEART

"Oh, give thanks to the LORD, for He is good! For His mercy endures forever. Let the redeemed of the LORD say so, Whom He has redeemed from the hand of the enemy..."(Ps. 107:1-2).

Every morning, from the time I was a toddler until my youth, my dad would wake me and my siblings up with a cheerful song called "Good Morning to You!" We looked forward to hearing his voice each morning before he left our home to begin his day. The melodious variations in his baritone voice filled our home with an awakening, inspiring surprise. From his heart to our hearts, the joy within him sent a sweet-smelling aroma that I will never forget.

Dad had a cheerful demeanor that sent a beautiful message to his family and to all who passed his way. Joy comes from the heart, and when it is expressed, people long to spend as much time with the one expressing it. Theodore Roosevelt said, "People don't care how much you know until they know first how much you care." Dad's awareness of everyone he surrounded made it easy to appreciate the knowledge he conveyed. He understood this quote to the max because he had compassion and gratitude for life. Jesus lived a life of compassion and love. Dad's song and sanguine personality let his family know he considered us each morning.

God is the same with his children. He says "hello!" and "good morning!" to us. He delights in His children. He gives breath and new mercies every morning. He wants us to delight in His sovereign will and share His message with others. Too often, we fall fast asleep from the time we are awakened. We wake up, but we close our eyes to His amazing love and new mercies. We walk by sight rather than by faith (2 Cor. 5:7). Therefore, our eyes are closed to His goodness and grace.

Let's be mindful that God, above all, is faithful to His people and should be forever worshiped. Psalm 107: 1-2 is a reminder that only the redeemed can truly celebrate who God is in their lives. God is always good! He is always merciful! He is always righteous! He is always just! He is the originator of love! Yes, we are forever His redeemed people. He never loses heart on our behalf, because He is God, and Jesus paid it all. Let's be cheerful and celebrate our God by knowing that every morning is a good morning.

So, Good Morning to You!

CONSIDER:

Upon waking up, ask the Lord to:

- ✓ Make Himself known to you in a special way.
- ✓ Give you a cheerful heart.
- ✓ Open your eyes so that you may see the beauty of His wonderful works in His entire creation.

LORD, help us to keep focused in knowing that it is never a dull morning in Christ. Help us to celebrate your goodness and your mercies each morning. Help us to let the world know that Jesus has saved us from the hand of our enemy. Help us to remember that it is always a good morning, because You are Sovereign! In Jesus' precious name, Amen.

JOURNAL #30

Is everyday a "Good Morning" for You? Can you remember someone who made you feel like life was promising and reminded you of God's presence?

Chapter Twenty-Seven

A JOYFUL HEART

"Rejoice in the Lord always, again I will say, rejoice" (Phil. 4:4)!"

Paul reminds the Philippian saints of their responsibility to honor the Lord by rejoicing in Him at all times. It is a pleasure to rejoice in the Lord, because He is our maker (Gen. 2:7) and has called us to His work (Eph. 2:10). We are united in Jesus as joint heirs (Rom. 8:17), so we serve with a joyful heart. Paul was concerned because there was a dispute between two women in the church at Phillipi. He said for them to be of the same mind (Phil.4:2) and spoke of oneness by having the mind of Christ (Phil. 2:5).

He also mentions that the church must hold these women accountable to God's word (vs. 3). Yes, accountability is necessary when our goal is to please the Lord. He challenges the church to conduct itself with gentleness, because people can become discouraged. Paul warned that prayer was the key toward unity. Unity in the church is a must if we are to draw others to Christ. People are turned off when they see Christians fighting against each other. It is a contradiction to our faith. Our purpose must take precedence over our differences. "To rejoice is the sphere in which the believer's joy exists-a sphere unrelated to the circumstances of life, but related to an unassailable, unchanging relationship to the sovereign Lord." We are heaven bound. Therefore, we must display grace, peace and our future hope.

Jesus Christ should always be the sphere of our influence. He is our focal point, and nothing should be placed above Him. Just as the Holy Spirit points the finger to Jesus Christ, we must always make him our reference, our source, our guide, our shield, our direction, our resolution, and our eternal hope. We must rise above our circumstances, by maintaining joy. So, "Rejoice in the Lord always, and again, I say Rejoice!"

CONSIDER:

- ✓ Are you rejoicing in what God is doing in your sphere of influence?
- ✓ Are you seeking God's wisdom when there are differences that you have no control over?

Lord, help us to have the mind of Christ so that all who are watching us will be changed and blessed by your presence in our lives. Help us to rejoice in the Lord because He is the reason we live. Help us to rise above our differences and our circumstances. In Jesus' name, Amen.

JOURNAL #31

What are ways you are rejoicing in the Lord for what He has done in your life?

Chapter Twenty-Eight

A HEART OF HOPE

"To them God willed to make known what the riches of the glory of this mystery among the Gentiles are: which is Christ in you, the hope of glory."

Paul's ministry was to the Gentiles, although he was of Hebrew origin and formerly persecuted and killed Christians. Saul was his name prior to his conversion. He was called by Jesus Christ on the way to Damascus to spread the "good news" (Acts 9). "This is why Paul could join the apostleship. Apostle means "'one who is sent…it primarily refers to the twelve men Christ chose to accompany Him and Matthias (Acts 1:15-26). Matthias was the apostle who had been chosen to replace Judas."

Keep in mind:

Paul was a Jewish man, but he was called to minister to the Gentiles. God calls, and we respond. Even if what He is calling us to do doesn't make sense to us, we must walk in obedience to His will. No one could stop Paul after he was called to minister to the Gentiles. He protected his call and contended for the faith. Be confident in your call. I'm sure Paul was known to all as a sell-out! Be a sell-out for Christ! Initially, even to the disciples, he was not to be trusted, but he walked worthy of his call, and over time, his sincere devotion to Christ proved itself.

Paul's purpose was to remind the Colossian Church that it was Christ in them who would make the difference in their lives. He fulfilled the law and the prophets (Matt. 5:17). "The Old Testament predicted the coming of the Messiah and that the Gentiles would partake of salvation." We see this in Isaiah 42:6 and 45:21, and in many other prophetic Scriptures. However, these believers did not realize that Christ would live in them. He would fulfill the call to righteousness in their lives. A word about Christ's complete work on the cross.

✓ Christ defeated the law and the prophets so that you would never have to compete with the Old Testament legalistic system. Jesus stands in place of our sins. The stain that sin left within us is cleared because of his sufferings, death, burial, and resurrection. He did it all by himself. Thank you, Lord!

✓ Christ's work on the cross also continues to satisfy us. He sets us apart from the world as we model his life and are transformed by the renewing of our minds (Rom. 12:2). So, you must be in the Word to be transformed by it!

What about the hope of Christ's glory? The hope we have in Christ Jesus will never end. God calls us. We embrace His call. Jesus continues the work, by the Holy Spirit who lives in us (Eph. 2). Remember he told his disciples that he would not leave them comfortless, but will send the Comforter, the Helper, the Holy Spirit (John 14: 18-26). Romans 5:3-8 says that God is working out His character in and through us. So, His glory is being revealed through us as we give Him our trials. It should inspire us to persevere through our suffering. Our hope in the Lord keeps us going, as we focus on God's love and the Spirit who leads us.

This profound hope in Christ doesn't end here on earth; it continues forever in the next life. 1 Corinthians 15:19-20 says, "If in this life only we have hope in Christ, we are of all men the most pitiable. But now Christ is risen from the dead and has become the first fruits of those who have fallen asleep.” Christ’s life was not in vain; therefore, our lives are not in vain. Since Christ has risen from the grave, we will live forever and meet Him in the air. He is our forever hope. Amen!

CONSIDER:

- ✓ Our faith in Christ increases by what we hear, see, and do.
- ✓ It is the Spirit of God who produces Christ-like character in us. We cannot live this life apart from the Holy Spirit. He dwells in every believer (1 Cor. 3:16), but we must be filled with the Spirit to maintain righteous living (Eph. 5:18).
- ✓ It is a mystery of what God will do. So, when you think you are defeated, remember that Paul was in chains, Jesus suffered at all costs, atoned your sins, and he was innocent. He is our hope. He qualifies us. He vindicates. He makes us shine.

Lord, help us to remember that the cross is our everlasting hope. Where sin abound, help us to receive your grace even more so. For your glory, honor, and praise. In Jesus' name, Amen.

JOURNAL #32

What are ways you are rejoicing in the Lord for what He has done in your life?

Chapter Twenty-Nine

A PRAYERFUL HEART

"The effective fervent prayer of a righteous man avails much" (James 5:16).

Oxford Languages Dictionary defines the word, effective, as "successful in producing a desired or intended result. The word, fervent, is defined as having or displaying a passionate intensity."

It was during the late 70s when my great-grandmother was sick and dying. My siblings and I were staying with our grandmother that weekend. My dear aunt, who had also lived there, asked us to fervently pray. We were taken into one bedroom to begin a nightly prayer vigil. We prayed intensely, and we were specific. We prayed according to what we were taught, to pray God's word. My aunt did not demand that we pray, but she desperately asked us to remain in constant prayer, believing that God would answer the heartfelt cry of seven children. She also prayed with hopes that God would restore my great-grandmother's health. God heard the intensity of our prayer, and our great-grandmother was miraculously healed.

My aunt was righteous, and she had faith in what God could do. She also knew that God would hear our prayers. Does God always respond with health and physical healing in this manner? Absolutely not! God physically heals whom He chooses (Rom. 9:18). Healing also occurs when a believer is taken to heaven. He or she is spiritually healed and forever present with the Lord. This is the ultimate healing that takes place when one knows the Lord. Whatever the healing, the bottom line is that God heals. God physically healed our grandmother, and we rejoiced.

CONSIDER:

- ✓ God hears the prayers of the pure in heart.
- ✓ He hears a child's prayer. (Matt. 19:14, Matt. 5:8)
- ✓ He hears the saint's prayer. (James 5:16, 1 Thess. 5:17)
- ✓ He hears a sinner's prayer for faith in Christ Jesus. (John 9:31)

Lord, help us to fervently pray about every period in life. Help us to remember that you alone have the power to heal the brokenhearted and those who are physically sick. Thank you, Lord, for allowing us to trust you with our lives, in Jesus' name Amen.

JOURNAL #33

Write about one desperate situation when you prayed earnestly to the Lord. If a past situation does not come to mind, write and pray to God about a recent situation that is mind-bottling. The Lord will respond. He is faithful!

Chapter Thirty

THE WISE HEART

Read Acts 1:15-26 for further context.
And they cast their lots, and the lot fell on Matthias. And he was numbered with the eleven apostles (Acts 1:26).

Jesus' ascension was a turning point for Peter, one of the disciples. You remember Peter, the impulsive, carnal disciple who fought violently trying to save Jesus from suffering the death of the cross by cutting off the Roman soldier's ear. His need for people's approval caused him shame and guilt before his peers and the world. This disciple had a change of heart after Jesus' ascension. He stepped up and, in humility, took leadership among 120 disciples of Christ in the upper room (v. 21-23). If you ever think God cannot use you, ask Him. He promises to use you for His glory and praise (Col. 3:17; 1 Cor. 6:20). You have purpose!

In this meeting place, the disciples discussed the son of perdition, Judas Iscariot, his betrayal, and his violent death by suicide. They also discussed replacing his role as a disciple of Christ with a twelfth person. FYI, the number twelve reminds us of the "tribes of Israel according to ancient tradition, which became naturally a favorite number among the Jews, especially as it carried with it the suggestion of Divine choice and Divine faithfulness. So, it figured in religious rituals, symbolism, and history."

Under Peter's leadership, the disciples chose four godly ways to choose the twelfth disciple, Matthias. First, they referred to the O.T. as a guide in supporting their decision to replace Judas' role. A few verses were shared from the Psalms regarding Judas, "Let his dwelling place be desolate, and let no one live in it...Let another take his office" (Ps. 69:25; Ps. 109:8). "The Greek word for office is 'episkopen,' meaning, a position of overseer." This counsel supported the idea that Judas' role needed to be replaced.

What are your first steps in making wise decisions?

CONSIDER:

- ✓ Why is there a decision needing to be made in this area and at this time?
- ✓ What Scriptures reinforce the need for change?
- ✓ Do you have God's peace?

Second, the person chosen would have to be mature in faith. This person had to identify with Jesus' former ministry with his disciples. As stated in verses 21-22, the man chosen must be taken from the one hundred and twenty men who had seen, heard, and witnessed Jesus' ministry. So, the person would need to have integrity, be a witness, and be dedicated to Christ. The passage states that all 120 men were with the disciples from John the Baptist's baptism to Jesus' ascension.

What is your second step in making wise decisions?

CONSIDER:

- ✓ Do you engage and consult like-minded God-fearing friends?
- ✓ What ministries or fellowships are you engaged in to help you mature in faith?
- ✓ Are you testifying about the goodness of the Lord?
- ✓ Is your spiritual walk consistent?
- ✓ Are you growing in faith and good character?

Third, prayer is essential when making important decisions. Heaven is open to God's people, and God speaks clearly as we lay our requests before Him. They proposed two men who were like-minded, Joseph called Barsabas and Matthias.

Their prayer comprised:

- ✓ Acknowledging God's sovereignty in knowing the hearts of men
- ✓ Acknowledging God's wisdom in knowing their individual hearts

What is your third step in making wise decisions?

CONSIDER:

- ✓ Do you offer your request to God for oneness and clarity?
- ✓ Do you have an even exchange of people who will pray with you concerning your decision?
- ✓ Do you pray that God's wisdom would exceed your earthly wisdom and wait for the right answer?

Fourth, they cast their lots to make the final call. Yes, they threw dice! Although this may seem secular, especially if it involves money. However, it was part of their decision-making process. Today, people throw dice for gambling purposes. We may also flip a coin, etc. It was customary for the Hebrews to cast lots to determine a specific outcome or to verify a decision. FYI, "A method of decision-making was used in ancient times to determine outcomes or make choices. It involved the random selection of an option or allocation of a task by drawing or throwing objects such as stones, dice, or marked sticks. The casting of lots was often employed in religious, legal, or communal contexts, including the allocation of land, the selection of leaders, or the division of spoils."

What are other methods people use to make spiritual decisions?

CONSIDER:

- ✓ Do you walk with blind faith? Or do you trust that your decision rests on God's providential care?
- ✓ Do you listen to the Spirit's still small voice in all matters? He may take you to a specific passage in Scripture to confirm your decision for change.
- ✓ Do you use the process of elimination? Yes, God is logical! He will clarify what changes need to be made and why.

The beautiful thing about serving the Lord is that we have options. We can pray that the Lord will bless our choices as guided by the process of life and the inclusion of spiritual resources. If we are wise about our decisions and willing to trust His guidance, we will hear from Him and experience His peace.

CONSIDER:

- ✓ How will you go on making present and future decisions?

Lord, help us to consult you about every decision we need to make. You are the Most High, all-powerful, and all-knowing God, full of wisdom and truth. Nothing takes you by surprise, so we gladly bring you our requests and glorify your name. In Jesus' name, Amen.

JOURNAL #34

What decisions are you contemplating?

How is God speaking to your heart about making wise decisions?

PART IV
LIFE REFRESHMENT

"Now the Lord is the Spirit; and where the Spirit of the Lord is, there is liberty/freedom" (2 Cor. 3:17).

Chapter Thirty-One

F-R-E-E-D-O-M IN HEART

A Life Goal!

Liberty is synonymous with the word freedom.
It is the state that "results from not being oppressed or in bondage."

The New Bible Dictionary notes:

> The biblical idea of liberty (freedom) has as its background the thought of imprisonment or slavery. Rulers would imprison those whom they regarded as wrongdoers (Gen. 39:20); a conquered nation might be enslaved by its conqueror, or a prisoner of war by his captor, or an individual might, like Joseph, be sold into slavery. When the Bible speaks of liberty, a prior bondage or incarceration is always implied. Liberty means the happy state of having been released from servitude for a life of enjoyment and satisfaction that was not possible before.

Freedom is the release of any form of control taken from a person's God-given identity. Where there is bondage, the presence and control of the Spirit are missing. On the other hand, those who are filled with the Spirit can soar above any yoke set to ensnare them. Although Paul was in prison and chained to a Roman soldier, he was free in the Spirit as a witness of Christ and messenger to the Church. He used his chains as an opportunity to serve Christ (Acts 28:16-20; Phil. 1:12-14). Even with his human disadvantages, as known by his life, he was purposeful and rose above his circumstances. I Peter 4:16 says, "Yet if anyone suffers as a Christian, let him not be ashamed, but let him glorify God in this matter." How does Paul's life speak to you?

Jesus is called the man of sorrow, yet he gracefully walked in obedience to the Father. He was nailed to the cross, and despite the opposition he faced, he continued to be faithful to his call. He, being God's Son, thought it not robbery to endure the cross for the sake of those who would someday trust in him (Phil.2). Thank you, Jesus!
How does Jesus' life speak to you?

The Lord allowed my grandmother to live on earth for ninety-four amazing years. However, at the age of ninety-two, a rare form of cancer was discovered in her body. She loved the Lord with all her heart and served him faithfully. Mindfully, the closer it became clearer that the cancer would take her life, she patiently waited to see her Lord. In her patience, she refused any medication because she did not want to be mentally numb to the environment. She desired to listen to the voices of her loved ones, even until her last breath. The sentimental reflections of past events, laughter, tears, and so forth were strengthening, despite her suffering. She knew that her heavenly home and perfect body were moments away. So, she made adjustments to be present with her family. As she breathed her last breath, so I was told, she quietly left this world into the arms of Jesus. She transitioned as she lived. She was free indeed!

God created man and woman in His image with the freedom to enjoy forever fellowship with Him (Gen. 2).

After the Fall, sin, sickness, and every form of evil reigned on the earth (Gen. 3). As Satan disguised himself in the form of a serpent in the Garden of Eden, he continues to disguise himself as the Angel of Light today. He is the adversary, the deceiver, the liar of all lies, and so forth. His desire is to "sift you as wheat" (Luke 22:31). Jesus is greater than any scheme, discomfort, or influence against us.

Increased freedom comes as we gaze at heaven in the direst times of our lives. Suffering, no matter what form, is detrimental to our physical, emotional, mental, and spiritual health. However, Scripture teaches us to run with patience, and to set our eyes on Jesus, the author and finisher of our faith (Heb. 12:1). Although life can be difficult, it is a process, and Jesus lived it perfectly for us. A person who has freedom in heart desires to be more like Jesus. Do you have a continual desire to be more like Jesus?

Galatians 5:1 reminds believers to stand firm in their freedom, because Christ has set us free from the law of sin and death. It concludes by saying, "Do not be entangled again with a yoke of bondage." The beauty of having freedom in Christ is that the Christian is victorious over any situation. Victorious living comprises the influence of the Holy Spirit. We can discern God's voice and walk circumspectly with wisdom, redeeming the time He has allotted us (Gal. 5:16-26). Never forget that those who exercise their freedom with purity of heart are free indeed.

The following pages are written to help one manage his or her heart properly. If freedom is a goal for you, consider using the acronym F-R-E-E-D-O-M, and keep in mind that Jesus offers ultimate freedom. He will return soon, and the believer's life will be changed forever! "So if the Son sets you free, you are free indeed" (John 8:36).

~Blessings upon Blessings!

Faith.

"But without faith it is impossible to please God, for He who comes to God must believe that He is, and that He is a rewarder of those who diligently seek Him" (Hebrews 11:6). Apart from faith in Christ, man is totally depraved. He is empty and will forever chase after what He cannot comprehend. Faith involves, first, the belief that God is who He says He is. It entails recognizing that man cannot please God based on his abilities. We come up short even on our best days. Imperfection can never equate perfection. It's like adding apples and oranges; it does not resolve itself. Man cannot obtain salvation by his works (Titus 3:5).

Faith=Belief
Recognize=Awareness
Engagement=Community
Endurance=Strength
Dignity=Respect
Opportunity=Observe
Manage=Time

Secondly, in approaching God, one must acknowledge His presence. To believe in God is to admit that He and His Son, Jesus, are one and of the same essence. Jesus' claims as God's Son on earth cost him his life. But the proof was in the resurrection. He rose, as he said he would, on the third day, which gives us complete faith and sustaining hope. "Most assuredly, I say to you, before Abraham was, I AM" (John 8:58). "I and My Father are one" (John 10:30).

Last, to increase our faith, one must believe that God keeps His promises. "God *is* not a man, that He should lie, nor a son of man, that He should repent. Has He said, and will He not do? Or has He spoken, and will He not make it good" (Num. 23:19)? In context, Balaam the prophet is speaking to Balak the king of Moab. Balak wanted Balaam to curse Israel because he feared their growing power. God, in return, told Balaam to speak what He says to His people, disavowing Balak's rule. The principle here is that God rules, and He never lies; what He says, He does. He can be trusted. He rewards those who diligently seek Him. If you have no faith, ask God for it. He will reveal Himself at any given time to those who willingly seek Him.

God desires to hear our deepest longings, feelings, hurts, wounds, and dissatisfactions. He wants us to share our hates and dislikes, mistreatments, misunderstandings, failures, anger, fears, joys, worries, reflections, sentiments of life, relationships, etc. Yes, everything! The point is that whatever you share, He can bear it, and He is faithful to respond. He already knows what's on your heart, but He desires to hear, heart to heart, from you.

Recognize.

To give recognition to something is to create awareness of it. Awareness is vital to experience freedom in heart. Awareness allows us to trade in our viewpoint and, in humility, recognize God's viewpoint. Without God's perspective, we lack wisdom and clarity in life. Isaiah, the prophet, saw the Lord while blinded by his own selfish human frailties. He set himself apart from the sins of the nation as if he were at the top of his game. That is, until the Lord opened his eyes to his own filthy heart through a vision, in the year that Uzziah, the king, had died (Is. 6).

Isaiah loved Uzziah and was called to be a prophet during his reign. However, even in his calling, he had weaknesses. God exposed his depraved heart, as his problem was his mouth. He came to realize he had the same struggles he had accused others of having, and his life was changed.

There are times when we open our mouths too much, and God must humble and quiet our spirits to make us aware of His presence and our sinful hearts. He desires church unity and peace among brothers and sisters in Christ. Chaos within one's heart creates confusion amid God's people, but when one recognizes his or her true purpose, God is pleased, and others will follow.

When Isaiah recognized his sin, an immediate and intimate awareness of God's presence set in. Self-centeredness and self-gratification went out the window and were replaced by God's complete viewpoint. If we are attentive, God will reveal the matters in our hearts. After losing Uzziah, Isaiah came to understand heaven more deeply and appreciatively. Heaven can be revealed to all who authentically open their hearts to the Lord.

Heaven guarantees awe and humility simultaneously. When God's presence is revealed, get ready, because the heart is being admirably transformed! "But we all, with unveiled faces, beholding as in a mirror the glory of the Lord, are being transformed into the same image from glory to glory, just as by the Spirit of the Lord" (2 Cor. 3:18). Our weaknesses expose us to God's heart. In his pain, Isaiah had a change of heart.

Even at the end of her life, Mom fastened her attention to heaven. She was in hospice, while at home. Although she had pain, she did not flinch. She gazed into Jesus's eyes, knowing her departure would soon come. She was in a fluctuating state of consciousness.

I will never forget when she called for me to sing one of her favorite songs that I used to sing around the house. It was called, "Rest in Me." Helen Baylor used to sing it on the radio, and the chorus lyrics are written below:

> Rest in Me, I am the lover of your soul. Rest in Me, I still have it all under control. I'm Alpha and Omega, the Beginning and Ending. I'm your heavenly Father; I still can provide. Rest in Me, I desire to bless you every day. Rest in Me, I can hear you each time that you pray. Yet, there are some things in this world that can stand in your way. All you have to do is be still and rest in me.

On this day in August 1996, I believe Mom desired to keep her heart aligned with God's will. I also believe that, as she selflessly lived, she considered my heart as well. She knew that I would need to keep my heart in check and depend totally on the Lord for the remainder of my life. I was soon to be married within a few months, at the time, and I would need every word of this song. Mom was humble and gracious, so considering her character, I believe that her intentions were for both of us. She consciously did not desire to be carried by the waves of this world while fixing her eyes on heaven. A perfect heart was soon to come for her, but for me, I would need to trust God that He would carry me through the storms of life.

Our sin nature exposes our need for increased faith in God. In recognition and awareness of His providence, promises, and provisions, we are humbled. Humility leads us to His grace and a need for others. I would dearly miss Mom's presence, but God wanted me to glean further into His presence.

Has someone been removed from your life to open your eyes and heart to God's presence?

Engagement.

"Alone we can do so little; together we can do so much."

Engagement with others is crucial for growth toward freedom. When God made Adam, He said that man should not be alone, so He pulled a rib from Adam and created Eve (Gen. 2:22). Community keeps us accountable and protects us from complacency and a victim complex. "Two are better than one, because they have a good reward for their labor. For if they fall, one will lift his companion, but woe to him who is alone when he falls, for he has no one to help him up" (Eccl. 4:9-10). Solomon discusses several advantages of a cohesive relationship. When married people work together in harmony, they benefit each other spiritually, emotionally, and even financially. Both bear the burden of ensuring that the family is well-nurtured and healthy.

The same is true for the body of believers. When we come together in fellowship and worship of our Lord, there is unity and peace. "Those who have both a strong relationship with God and strong friendships with other believers will have bonds that strengthen life's joys and limit life's sorrows."

Be reminded of the first-century church as described in Acts 2. The power they exuded came from the Holy Spirit, which unified them. They practically lived together (Acts 2:42-47)! We desire their results but fail to use their methods. Engagement with others allows for freedom through transparency, challenge, and creativity. I have been, at most, lonely when I have pulled myself away from the body of believers. My limited reasoning was not as critical as my obedience to God. Paul speaks of brokenness within the body of Christ when everyone is not involved (1 Cor. 12:15-19). Our need for one another is vital in our spiritual development and our witness. Have you ever felt separated from the community of believers and experienced an emotional and spiritual void? "For to be carnally minded is death, but to be spiritually minded is life and peace" (Romans 8:6). What have you missed in life when you have been absent from the community of believers?

Endurance.

"It always seems impossible until it's done."

Have you ever had high hopes for a change that was entering your life, but to your surprise, nothing seemed to have turned out the way you expected? The only thing that brought peace and stability was God's presence. I returned to school soon after my husband and I relocated to Texas. I decided to endure life no matter what came my way. I diligently worked hard, with hopes of a great future. I met great people, and God blessed my studies.

During the first trimester of our daughter's conception, I had what is called Hyperemesis Gravidarum. This devastating illness had made me sick for the entire 1st trimester of pregnancy, which led to my withdrawal from school. It took me a while to regain strength and feel healthy again. However, I waded through the pregnancy and later returned to school, but during my second pregnancy, the illness returned. At this time, I was in my fourth year of schooling but could not keep up with my studies. Therefore, I had to withdraw once again.

After having two children and moving to another city, I eventually completed my undergraduate studies. What God stirred up within me academically in my early twenties, he continued throughout the years. I have learned to endure whatever life brings. There have been many tests, but He has proven Himself faithful every time.

Grieving the loss of my very best sister-friend left me a bit saddened. We had been friends for thirty-six years. She had experienced depression beyond my imagination. Before I moved to Texas, both of us had gone through a church split at the same time, and we had thrown temper tantrums about it. Yes, adult temper tantrums, literally! Have you been there? Neither of us was prepared for this type of church dysfunction. We were broken, but God was carrying us. Have you had the feeling where God's mighty arms were holding you tightly? During my particular church split, a remnant of godly people prayed and fasted while supporting one another. Whereas my great sister-friend felt alone in her church situation.

Two years later, my husband and I were leaving Pennsylvania to relocate to Texas, as we had planned three years prior to our marriage. However, she remained in her situation. Her father had died years prior to her church split, her mother died years later, and her brother had relocated to another state. She had slowly declined and pulled away from family members and the church scenery due to heartbreak, fear, and emotional and spiritual decline. She ended up having a mental breakdown, which led to the psychological disorder agoraphobia.

In her book, *You Are More Than You Know, Face Your Fears, Grow Stronger,* comedian Patsy Clairmont describes her past situation with having agoraphobia. She says,

> "I was an agoraphobic-afraid of open spaces and crowds of people. I was afraid of doctors, hospitals, medicine, elevators, heights, tunnels, bridges, people's opinions, just to name a few…'Fear suggests that it came on suddenly when it's been setting up housekeeping inside of us most of our lives.' Satan has just been waiting for a situation where he would catch us off guard and set off fear explosives."

He surely set off "fear explosives" in my friend's life. However, as Patsy recovered, my great friend never improved. Her fears led to deeper wounds, and she died of a heart attack at just fifty-nine years old.

After her death, I praised God many times for godly preservation and the desire to never give up. Placing myself in her shoes, I could have been in the same predicament without the support of family and friends. "...and not only that, but we also glory in tribulations, knowing that tribulation produces perseverance, and perseverance, character, and character, hope. Now hope does not disappoint, because the love of God has been poured out in our hearts by the Holy Spirit who was given to us" (Rom. 5:3-5). The believer's future hope allows one to persevere, knowing that God's character is being developed in us, and earth is not a dead end. There is victory on the other side.

God's keeping power sustains us even when we cannot see the light at the end of the tunnel. I can only wish that my great friend had understood how to confront her deepest fears, but God chose to extend to her His ultimate healing because of His love and grace. How have you endured the trials that have seemed most unbearable? If you feel like you are being swallowed up in the quicksand of life, hang in there, and call on the name of the Lord. He will rescue you!

Dignity.

You are worthy of respect.

After creating the world, God declared that everything He had made was good (Gen. 1:31). God created us with dignity. When we truly understand God's promises and His perspective of us, we see the world through different lenses. We shake off the dust of control from within and without and have a change of heart. As our relationship with Christ matures, we move further into His purpose because it becomes increasingly clear and natural to us. We walk as He speaks. We are in step with His Spirit (Eph. 1:14). No one must tell us how to display our faith and the values that are dear to our hearts. We are who He created us to be, when His voice is clear in us.

Dorothy Mae Ballard was her name. She walked, talked, and lived as if life would never end. Her life demonstrated future expectancy. She was an elementary school teacher and my fabulous godmother. Nothing could stop her from living life with purpose. She made life look so easy, although her struggles were obvious. She had been teaching for almost thirty years before her death. Her electrifying smile and mesmerizing, melodious voice were captivating. She spoke calmly and softly. The Lord was with her. She could not be moved and had unshakable faith.

Her last day on earth came like a flood from rivers of water. As she prepared to teach her elementary school class one morning, she called me, left a message, and stated she loved me. We would talk at least three times a week, prior to this call, usually at 5:00 a.m., before I relocated. I received several messages stating that she had been trying to contact me. I was in orientation at Texas State University at the time. I called her, and she was at the hospital. Her voice sounded as usual, energetic and high-pitched. Most likely because she did not want to alarm me. Even if she was hurting, she never panicked in my presence. She was always calm, cool, and collected, specifying that everything would be okay. She said, "just a minute." As I momentarily waited on the phone, suddenly, a nurse came into the room. She said in her upbeat voice, "Gotta go!", Gotta go!" I had no clue that day would be the last time we talked. My heart felt like an elephant had sat on it when I heard the news that she had suddenly left this earth. I was crushed! And Distraught!

However, when I thought about her feelings at that present state and for all eternity, she transitioned to heaven as she lived on earth. Free as a bird! She had been ultimately healed. "Strength and honor are her clothing; she shall rejoice in times to come" (Prov. 31:25). I look forward to seeing her and others someday again.

Life is not about what you wear! It is about what wears YOU! Dignity is not something you put on, it is what comprises you. I am reminded of women in the Church who wear their absolute best, but their hearts are far away from the Lord. God has granted us gifts and abilities to use for His glory, and dignity complements it all. He has placed many women with a special calling in my life. Even today, although a few are deceased, I continue to reflect on how they lived with passion for Christ, and I draw from their lives. Today, I am still meeting women of purpose who are touching my life. No one must point out their God-given worth. They follow the Holy Spirit's voice and yield to His call. They wear their gifts well, and dignity encompasses their being. They walk with grace, wisdom, and joy, and they forever count their blessings. May we always count our blessings, naming them one by one.

One of the rewarding benefits of having children and raising them into adulthood is that they can testify and delight in their mother's dignified manners. In the quietness of the home, they remember things that she has forgotten. They speak of the good old times and present situations that continue to stretch and strengthen their lives. Dignity encompasses those who walk in faith and look forward to the future, knowing that God covers it all! "It means a belief in oneself, that one is worthy of the best. It means that what I have to say is important, and I will say it when it's important for me to say it. Dignity really means that I deserve the best treatment I can receive. And that I have the responsibility to give the best treatment I can to other people." This type of dignity does not come with pride or privilege. It is quiet, humble, and inspiring.

Where has dignity shown up in your life?
Who are the women that has inspired you mostly?
If you cannot think of one, ask the Lord, who? He will show you or place one in your life.

Opportunity.

With Dignity comes opportunity.

"In every human soul is a God-given awareness that there is 'something more' than this transient world. And with that awareness of eternity comes a hope that we can one day find a fulfillment not afforded by the 'vanity' in this world." When you realize that you are beyond any circumstance, you move with greater purpose. God is larger than life. He predestined your future before your existence. "When I was made in secret, and skillfully wrought in the lowest parts of the earth. Your eyes saw my substance, being yet unformed. And in Your book they all were written, the days fashioned for me, when as yet there were none of them" (Ps. 139:15-16). Thank God for the reality of this principle. As we walk in the flow of life, God presents us with opportunities. We must be presently aware and sensitive to the Holy Spirit's small, still voice. "My sheep hear My voice, and I know them, and they follow Me" (John 10:27).

I will never forget the time I was in the market. A lady had left her cart sitting in an aisle with her purse inside. She seemed distressed, as I remember her face and mannerisms. The purse was open, and I really didn't want to touch it, but it seemed she must have mistakenly taken my cart, subconsciously thinking it was hers. I ended up finding my cart in another aisle sitting alone, but I could not find this woman. I knew if I had left her cart in the aisle, someone would have stolen her purse. On the other hand, I thought, "what if she catches me moving her cart, with her purse in it?" She could accuse me of stealing her purse. It was risky, but I took the chance. I took the cart to customer service, explained the situation, and left it in their care. I had no clue what happened to her that day, but I prayed that she had found her purse within the store's protection.

On another occasion, when I would homeschool my kids at the library, there was a heavy-set woman with snow-white hair who would come every Thursday morning. She was older and retired, but we would have great conversations while there. One Thursday morning, as the kids and I came out of the car, she took her time getting out of her car, as she sat in a designated handicapped space. I thought, "I hope she is okay." When she saw me, she said hello, but her breathing was delayed. I asked her if she needed help, and she replied, "Yes." I helped her get out of the car, and she walked very slowly into the library, grabbed my hand tightly, and said, "Thank you, dear sister! All things are possible to them who believe." I responded with a quiet "amen" and prayed for her. After that day, I looked for her but never saw her again. I often wondered if that was her last day on earth. I thanked God for the opportunity to know and help her and continued to appreciate those special moments in life.

The Holy Spirit makes us aware of occurrences where we must act on another's behalf. "But the Helper, the Holy Spirit, whom the Father will send in My name, He will teach you all things and bring to your remembrance all things that I said to you" (John 14:26). There have been numerous opportunities presented for me to opened myself to God's will. It is the small things that seem to go unnoticed. Who knows, both women could have been His daughters, too. That makes me smile.

Are you aware of God's presence in your life? How about in the workplace, home, marketplace, etc.?
Has He presented any special opportunities to you, lately?

Manage Your Time.

"Redeem the time, because the days are evil" (Eph. 5:16).

"Time denotes a fixed, measured, allocated season with the definite article 'the,' it likely refers to one's lifetime as a believer. We are to make the most of our time on this evil earth in fulfilling God's purposes, lining up every opportunity for useful worship and service." I have never seen a man pack so much into his schedule and fulfill it all. A husband, dad, student, pastor, friend, and diligent worker. He has fulfilled many responsibilities since we were married, and most importantly, has been there for most of our commitments, every milestone for our children, including sports activities, fine arts, etc. despite his demanding schedule.

His name is Greg. He is one of a kind. He is a man of integrity who desires to be more like Jesus by walking in his character and relying on His strength, even when life seems unbearable. He loves to minister through God's Word to encourage the saints, and has impacted many lives, both at work and within the church community. Being the center of our family, I pray for his health, emotionally, physically, mentally, and spiritually. God has always come through for our family as he has considered Him. "For the eyes of the Lord run to and fro throughout the whole earth, to show Himself strong on behalf of those whose heart is loyal to Him" (2 Chr. 16:9). Our family is blessed, and we value Greg's presence.

Time. "So, teach us to number our days, that we may gain

a heart of wisdom" (Ps. 90:12). So often, we fall prey to the demands of cultural norms. However, prioritizing our days is extremely important because we never know what will come in a day. We can alleviate our frustrations if we are attentive to the godly principles of time. The Bible teaches us to pray without ceasing because time never stands still (1 Thess. 5:17). I try to keep in mind that God is not slow to His promises (2 Peter 3:9). Therefore, "delay" is not in His vocabulary. We must be wise in our choices and not spend our time on other people's biases, opinions, and projections.

Social media can be beneficial, but it can also be harmful, as it can be a smooth deception that steals our valuable time. I joined Facebook in 2008, but shortly after, I quickly realized it was not the platform for me. My life was filled with other demands, and I needed to make the most out of my time.

About four years ago, I returned to social media, convinced it was the right time. Twenty-twenty had come, and many people had died. I wanted to see how family members and others from my past were progressing in life. Today, I am feeling obligated to maintain complete focus once again. Periodically, I check in to see what's going on, and it has been wonderful to see how God is blessing His people.

I am an early riser and have an exercise regimen. I am also a business owner and a student. I have also worked and volunteered, along with church activities. Managing my time properly has been challenging at times, but I praise God for the support of my husband, my children, my extended family members, and my extraordinary church family.

Keep in mind the acronym: F-R-E-E-D-O-M
If you desire true freedom, have **FAITH** that God is who He says He is. Trust His character and promises. Pray for awareness of His presence, in **RECOGNITION** that He meets us where we are. **ENGAGE** within a Bible teaching community and never isolate yourself. God desires to use you, and the faith community needs you. "**ENDURE** hardship as a good soldier of Christ" (2 Tim. 2:3). Walk with **DIGNITY**. God sees you through His loving eyes, and nothing or no one can ever change the love He has for His people. Pray for **OPPORTUNITY** and listen as the Holy Spirit leads you. Finally, never fail to **MANAGE** and minimize time spent on anything that hinders or distracts you from spiritual development. You are victorious! You are the child of the King! Give attention to your heart and purify it before the Lord and He promises to give you His upmost desires (Ps. 37:4-paraphrased).

Spence, a prolific commentator writes Psalms 37:4 this way:

> **Delight thyself also in the Lord**. Draw from communion with God all that inward intensity of joy which it is capable of giving. **And he shall give thee the desires of thine heart.** God will then grant thee all thy desires, and make thee perfectly happy.

God will guide you into His will, in spirit and in heart. So, take care of your heart. Heart Management is for YOU!

If *Heart Management* has encouraged or inspired you, please consider leaving a review on Amazon.com. Your feedback is greatly appreciated—thank you for your support!

NOTES

Preface

1.Roy T. Bennett, quote, https://www.goodreads.com/quotes/tag/enjoy-the-journey.

Heart Management: Introduction

1. Robert Jamieson, A. R. Fausset, and David Brown, *Commentary Critical and Explanatory on the Whole Bible*, vol. 1 (Oak Harbor, WA: Logos Research Systems, Inc., 1997), 392.
2.“A heart aligned with God is a life aligned with purpose,” author unknown.”

Chapter 1: The Heart

1. Maya Angelou, quote, Wisdom to Inspire the Soul, https//wisdomtoinspirethesoul.com/2014/10/mayaangelou.

Chapter 2: Authentic Hearts

1. Dr. William Krispin, *Christ at the Wall in the City: The Life and Ministry of Bill Krispin* (New Cumberland, PA: Honeycomb House Publishing LLC, 2024).

Chapter 3: Declutter Your Heart, Declutter Your Life

1. Peter Walsh, quote, Pinterest, http://www.pinterest.com/pin/131730357838434736/.
2. Ken Gire, *The Reflective Life* (Colorado Springs, CO Chariot Victor Publishing, 1998).
3. Sheila Walsh, quotes, Goodreads, https://www.goodreads.com/author/quotes/21763.Sheila.Walsh4. Robert Jeffress, *When Forgiveness Doesn’t Make Sense* (New York, NY: WaterBrook, 2019).

5. Maria Shriver, *I've Been Thinking* (New, JY: Penguin Random House, 2018).
6. Sheila Walsh, *It's Okay Not to Be Okay* (Grand Rapids, MI: Baker Books, 2018).
7. Austin Kleon, quote, QuoteFancy, https://quotefancy.com/quote/1720386.
8. Henry Cloud and John Townsend, *Boundaries* (Grand Rapids, MI: Zondervan, 2017).
9. John F. Kennedy, quote, BrainyQuote, https://www.brainyquote.com/quotes/john.f.kennedy105511.
10. Kenneth C. Haugk, Joel P. Bretscher, and Robert A. Musser, *Caring Assertiveness* (St. Louis, MO: Stephen Ministries, 2024).
11. A.T. Robertson, *Word Pictures in the New Testament* (Nashville, TN: Broadman Press, 1933), Mt 18:21.
12. Don Colbert, Ph.D, *Deadly Emotions* (Nashville, TN: Thomas Nelson, 2003).

Chapter 4: Identity in Heart

1. Marcus Warner, *Breakthrough,* (Chicago, I: Moody Publishers, 2024).
2. Angela Carwheel, quote, Excel Life Coaching for Women, 2024, https://www.excellifecoachingforwomen.com.

Chapter 5: A Grieving Heart

1. Gary R. Collins, *Chistian Counseling* (Wheaton, IL, Zondervan, 2007).
2. Georgia Shaffer, *A Gift of Mourning Glories* (Friendswood, TX: Bold Vision Books, 2017).

Chapter 6: A Contented Heart

1. Gaspard Cardinal Mermillod, analysis, Bartleby, https://www.bartleby.com/essay/Analysis-Of-Gaspard-Mermillod-s-Nasrin-FKWJ9RVK6ZKW.

Chapter 7: An Intentional Heart

1. Henry Cloud and John Townsend, *Boundaries* (Grand Rapids, MI: Zondervan, 2017).
2. Sheila Walsh, quotes, Goodreads, https://www.goodreads.com/author/quotes/21763.Sheila.Walsh

Chapter 8: A Deliberate Heart

1. Angela Carwheel, quote, Excel Life Coaching for Women, 2024, https://www.excellifecoachingforwomen.com.

Chapter 10: An Authentic Heart

1. Oxford English Dictionary, s.v. "value," https://www.oed.com/search/dictionary/?scope-Entries&q=value.
2. Albert Einstein, quote, Goodreads, https://www.goodreads.com/quotes/8906892.

Chapter 11: A Surrendered Heart

1. John MacArthur, *The MacArthur Study Bible* (Nashville, TN: Thomas Nelson, 1997).

Chapter 12: An Assured Heart

1. Socrates, quote, QuoteFancy, https://quotefancy.com/quote/758511.
2. https://quotes.lifehack.org/authors/michael_jordan.
3. Carol S. Dweck, Ph.D., *Mindset, The New Psychology of Success* (New York, NY: Ballantine Books, 2016).

Chapter 13: Purpose in Heart

1. John MacArthur, *The MacArthur Study Bible* (Nashville, TN: Thomas Nelson, 1997).

Chapter 14: Fear – Where Are You?

1. Don Colbert, Ph.D, *Deadly Emotions* (Nashville, TN: Thomas Nelson, 2003).
2. G. Campbell Morgan, quote, Daily Christian Quote, https://www.dailychristianquote.com/g-campbell-morgan-21/.
3. Dr. David Jeremiah, Turning Point Ministries, *Suffering.* https://www.youtube.com/watch?v=-VLg3CHiV6k (August 16, 2024).

Chapter 15: Controlling Your Heart

1. June Hunt, *Thoughts and Emotions* (Dallas, TX: Hope for the Heart, 2022).
2. Gary R. Collins, *Christian Counseling* (Wheaton, IL: Zondervan, 2007).
3. Gary Chapman, quote, Goodreads, https://www.goodreads.com/work/quotes/1936420-handling-a-powerful-emotion-ina-healthy-way.

Chapter 16: Training Your Heart

1. Don Colbert, *Deadly Emotions* (Nashville, TN: Thomas Nelson, 2003).
2. June Hunt, *Worry* (Peabody, MA: Aspire Press, 2021).

Chapter 18: A Heart Aligned with God

1. Ronald Youngblood, Editor: *Nelson's New Illustrated Bible Dictionary* (Nashville, TN: Thomas Nelson Publishers, 1995, 1986).
2. Dr. David Jeremiah, *The Jeremiah Study Bible* (Brentwood, TN: Worthy Publishing, Inc., 2013).

3. John MacArthur, *The MacArthur Study Bible* (Nashville, TN: Thomas Nelson, 1997).

Chapter 19: A Friend in Heart

1. J.H. Bernard, *A Critical and Exegetical Commentary on the Gospel According to St. John,* 633.

Chapter 24: A Conscientious Heart

1. James A. Brooks, Mark, vol.23, *The New American Commentary* (Nashville: Broadman & Holman, 1991), 152.
2. Rodney I. Cooper, Mark, vol. 2, *Holman New Testament Commentary* (Nashville: Broadman & Holman, 2000), 152.
3. John D. Barry et al., *Faithlife Study Bible* (Bellingham, WA: Lexham Press, 2012, 2016), Mk 9:42.

Chapter 26: A Good Heart

1. Quote, Goodreads, https://www.goodreads.com/quotes/34690.

Chapter 27: A Joyful Heart

1. John MacArthur, *The MacArthur Study Bible* (Nashville, TN: Thomas Nelson, 1997).

Chapter 28: A Heart of Hope

1. John MacArthur, *The MacArthur Study Bible* (Nashville, TN: Thomas Nelson, 1997).

Chapter 29: A Prayerful Heart

1.https://www.google.com/search?q=effectivehttps://www.google.com/search?q=fervent+definition&scaesv+b37190038783f505&sxsrf.

Chapter 30: The Wise Heart

1. *A Dictionary of Christ and the Gospels,* Logos Bible Software.
2. *The Care and Counsel Bible* (Nashville, TN: HarperCollins Christian Publishing, 2001).

Chapter 31: Freedom in Heart

1. *The Care and Counsel Bible* (Nashville, TN: HarperCollins Christian Publishing, 2001).
2. Patsy Clairmont, *You Are More Than You Know* (Franklin, TN: Worthy Books, 2015).
3. John MacArthur, *The MacArthur Study Bible* (Nashville, TN: Thomas Nelson, 1997).
4. "*Eternity in Our Hearts,*" Got Questions Ministries, https://www.gotquestions.org/eternity-in-our-hearts.html.
5. J.I.Packer, *The New Bible Dictionary,* 3rd ed. (Downers Grove, IL: InterVarsity Press), 684-686.
6. MayaAngelou, quote, Wisdom to Inspire the Soul, https://wisdomtoinispirethesoul.com/2014/10/mayaangelou.
7. Nelson Mandela, quote, https://quoteinvestigator.com/2016/01/05/done/.
8. Helen Keller, quote, https://quoteinvestigator.com/2014/04/21/together/.
9. H. D. M. Spence-Jones, ed., *Psalms*, vol. 1, The Pulpit Commentary (London; New York: Funk & Wagnalls Company, 1909), 285.

About the Author

Angela has been married to her husband, Greg, for 29 years and is the mother of two children, Genesis and Alexander, as well as her dog named Wesscott. She is the founder of Excel Life Coaching for Women, LLC, and faithfully serves in her church community.

Angela is currently pursuing a Doctor of Educational Ministry (DEdMin) at Dallas Theological Seminary, with a concentration in Coaching, Mentoring, and Discipleship. She is passionate about helping individuals experience both emotional and spiritual healing by addressing the heart through biblical truth and practical, compassionate guidance.

Angela also holds a Master of Theological Studies and a Master of Arts in Christian Education, specializing in Biblical Counseling, from Southwestern Baptist Theological Seminary, as well as a Bachelor of Arts in Psychology. Since 1996, she has been a certified Biblical Counselor through Christian Research and Development (CRD), helping women pursue emotional healing and restoration.

Angela is a Certified Christian Life Coach and Grief Coach, and she serves as a GriefShare facilitator. She is an active member of the International Christian Coaching Institute, the International Christian Coaching Association, and the International Association of Biblical Counselors.

Contact Angela at:
info@excellifecoachingforwomen.com

www.ingramcontent.com/pod-product-compliance
Lightning Source LLC
LaVergne TN
LVHW010653110826
845149LV00014B/3068

* 9 7 9 8 9 9 9 3 9 8 3 1 4 *